The Blue Bombers

The True Story of the 2009 Little League World Champions

By

WADE LINDENBERGER & MIKE FORD

ALSO BY WADE LINDENBERGER & MIKE FORD

Brotherhood of the Pigskin: A Fantasy Football Novel

Praise for the Book and the Team

"Our national pastime and the American Dream in one story."
George Lopez—Comedian and actor

"The Blue Bombers' extraordinary championship season excited and inspired the entire community. We have been proud to honor them all season long at PETCO Park, and we are excited to celebrate this new book, which will give us a behind-the-scenes glimpse at a season that reminded us all just how magical baseball can be."
Tom Garfinkel—President and COO of the San Diego Padres

"Rarely does a team of teenagers encounter a chance to ascend to the very pinnacle of their sport while also elevating the spirits of their community. Chula Vista's Park View Little League did exactly that in the summer of 2009. The Blue Bombers have set the bar for the rest of San Diego. A world championship is a glorious thing, and Park View was more than generous in sharing their triumph. Thanks guys."
Billy Ray Smith—The Scott and BR Show on XX 1090 Sports Radio and former NFL All-Pro

"I can't think of anything sweeter than the sounds of Little League baseball and the dream that all boys have to play in Williamsport, PA late in August. Park View Little League brought all of San Diego to their feet in 2009 with a World Series win and no one was happier for them than me and my Northern Little League teammates, who brought the only other Championship to the San Diego Area in 1961. Well done, boys. This book gives us a chance to experience those thrilling moments all over again."
Brian Sipe—1961 Little League World Series Champion and 1980 National Football League MVP

*To kids around the world who dream of some day
representing their hometown and playing
in Williamsport, Pennsylvania, for a chance
to become the Little League World Series Champions.*

Table of Contents

Acknowledgments ix

Foreword xi

Prologue xiii

Chapter 1 1

Chapter 2 8

Chapter 3 21

Chapter 4 32

Chapter 5 43

Chapter 6 53

Chapter 7 60

Chapter 8 67

Chapter 9 74

Chapter 10 86

Epilogue 101

Appendix: Recap of Tournaments 107

Sources 113

Notes 117

Index 133

The 2009 Park View Little League "Blue Bombers"

Players:

Andy Rios, SS-P
Kiko Garcia, CF-LF-P
Luke Ramirez, LF-1B-P
Bulla Graft, 2B
Bradley Roberto, RF
Oscar Castro, 1B-3B-P
Daniel Porras Jr., C
Isaiah Armenta, P-LF-PH
Markus Melin, CF
Nick Conlin, LF-CF-RF
Seth Godfrey, 3B-SS
Jensen Peterson, C

Coaches:

Oscar Castro, Manager
Ric Ramirez, Coach

Board of Directors:

Rod Roberto, President
Alex Marmolejo, VP of Administration

Russell Godfrey, VP of Operations
Jonalee Inzunza, Player Agent
Hope Marmolejo, Secretary
Mike McNaughton, Equipment Officer
Jim Withrow, Field Maintenance
Shelly Garcia, Concessionaire
Steve Myers, Safety Officer
Jerry Warmkessel, Information Officer
Mike Zizzi, Treasurer
Jeff Norton, Chief Umpire
Jaime Dorado, Chief Scorekeeper
Elva Lopez-Zepeda, Sponsorship

Acknowledgments

For 2 weeks in the summer of 2009, millions of fans throughout the world were focused on the youth version of America's favorite pastime—Little League baseball. As teams from California to Chinese Taipei and all points in between gathered in Williamsport, Pennsylvania, for the Little League World Series, only one team would raise the trophy in victory. Park View Little League from Chula Vista, California, mesmerized the world with their unique brand of baseball and made the championship their own. We were part of the millions who watched the home run record-breaking accomplishment of the apt-named Blue Bombers. When it was over, we knew we needed to tell this story to the world.

Now that we have completed *The Blue Bombers: The True Story of the 2009 Little League World Champions*, we would like to acknowledge some of the people who helped us during the process.

Many of our talented friends graciously reviewed the first draft of this book and provided excellent input that resulted in significant changes to the content and order in the final draft—Tom Chintala, Nancy Paznokas, Korrin Main, Kathy Baranowski, Ira Gershow, Teresa Warren, Scott Malkoff, Anne and Carolyn Ford, and Kayoko Lindenberger. Teresa also provided stellar PR support.

Terry Melia at Upper Deck gave us access to the fabulous trading cards of the boys and coaches that grace Chapters 2 and 3. Jane

Mitchell at Channel 4 San Diego hosts the oft-awarded show *One on One with Jane Mitchell*. She took time out of her very busy schedule to provide us with some valuable input on the team and the literary process. Patrick Schneeman, Sweetwater's coach, and Brent Rhylick, Rancho Santa Margarita's coach, gave us a couple of great interviews and an insider's perspective on the Park View team.

Rod Roberto said "yes" to our request to write this book and worked closely with us to make it a reality. The players' parents donated their time, recollections, and photographs, and supported our efforts to gather information from and interview their children, in particular Sharon Garcia, who reviewed a draft of the book and provided insightful comments. Mike McNaughton, a perennial board member of Park View Little League, along with Danny Vega, an early coach and long-time supporter of the League, spent an afternoon with us reminiscing about the early days of Park View and provided some great material for the book that would have otherwise been unavailable to us. We are especially appreciative of the extra time Manager Oscar Castro and Coach Ric Ramirez put in to complete our research. We are also thankful for the tireless all-purpose support of Andy Rios Sr., who is definitely a candidate for MVP in our book. Of course, this book is all about the kids, and we are grateful not only for the time they gave us during the process of completing this book, but for the excitement they brought to our lives and the great example they provide to other kids out there—it was a wonderful trip, Andy, Kiko, Luke, Bulla, Bradley, Oscar, Daniel, Isaiah, Markus, Nick, Seth, and Jensen.

Of course, we could not have done this without our families, who endured the time we spent on the book after-hours and on weekends, reviewed drafts, and sounded out ideas—the Fords—Anne, Andrew, Daniel, Elizabeth, and Carolyn—and the Lindenbergers—Kayoko, Paula, and Max. We love you and thank you for your awesome support during the past 12 months.

Foreword

Timing is everything, especially in sports.

The timely hit, the quarterback sack to end a drive, the buzzer-beater on the hardwood—all serve as those moments in sports that live forever in our hearts and minds.

Rarely does a team of teenagers encounter a chance to ascend to the very pinnacle of their sport while also elevating the spirits of their community.

Chula Vista's Park View Little League did exactly that in the summer of 2009.

Maybe it's because we all have some Little League baseball memories. Whether playing the game or cheering on the players, Little League baseball is good for the soul. It is the purest form of the Great American Pastime.

The Blue Bombers did something that is rare for a San Diego sports team—they won it all.

The Chargers have appeared in the Super Bowl, and the Padres have made it to two World Series. But neither rose to the occasion like Park View.

It was one of the great moments for us at XX 1090 Sports Radio. We allowed the players, coaches, and parents total access to the airwaves of Southern California.

To interview anyone from Park View (player, coach, mom, or dad, for that matter) while the team was plowing through the competition lessened the distance from Williamsport to San Diego and drew the entire community into the drama.

By the way, the kids were still kids when it was all over—a phenomenal dugout of baseball phenoms, and dedicated parents, and coaches that were doing it all for the love of the game.

The Blue Bombers have set the bar for the rest of San Diego. A world championship is a glorious thing, and Park View was more than generous in sharing their triumph.

These kids will soon transition into adulthood, and I hope that they never forget the lessons of 2009.

Anything can happen.

Thanks, guys.

Billy Ray Smith
The Scott and BR Show
XX 1090 Sports Radio

Prologue

"Little League baseball is a very good thing because it keeps the parents off the streets."
—Yogi Berra, Hall of Fame New York Yankee catcher[1]

The World Series Championship flag now flies proudly over the Park View Little League stadium. In the 2009 Little League Baseball World Series, the coaches of the Park View team from Chula Vista, California, piloted their talented young players to the pinnacle of youth baseball. Almost 200,000 teams started this journey,[2] yet only one made it to the finish line. Over Park View's magical run, they won 23 games and lost just three in 2 months of tournament ball. A national television audience saw Park View pound team after team in San Bernardino during the West Regional Tournament, where they went 6–0 and outscored their opponents 98–15, earning the nickname "the Green Machine" because of the color of their Park View Little League All-Star uniforms. When they arrived in Williamsport, Pennsylvania, they traded green for baby blue, and opened up with a 15–0 win against the Great Lakes team from Kentucky and followed up with a 14–0 win against the team from New England. During their 26-game drive to the Little League World Series Championship, the team smashed 104 home runs, prompting the media to compare them to the New York Yankees' Bronx Bombers and earning the label that will describe them forever—the Blue Bombers.

There have been 62 previous winners of the World Series,[3] so why is this victory so special? Because the team worked hard and maintained focus while relaxing and having fun. A study by the National

Alliance for Youth Sports found that 70 percent of American kids who sign up for sports quit by the time they are 13 because they aren't having fun anymore. The reason? Many parents take youth sports too seriously and place undue emphasis on winning.[4] Little League is no stranger to this. The 12 and under version of the national pastime has morphed from its humble beginnings in 1938 to the world's largest organized youth sports program, with over 2.3 million participants from more than 80 countries.[5] Each year, it culminates in the World Series. The Championship game alone attracted 3.9 million viewers for ABC.[6] Little League is big business, which intensifies the pressure on our young players to win.

The Park View team won the championship while being largely shielded from that pressure. The championship was very important to them, but they never lost perspective, and they never forgot to have fun along the way. Perhaps it came easier for them because of their camaraderie and history together, as many of the boys had been teammates since the age of 5.

As Luke Ramirez, the 6-foot-2, 212-pound Park View pitcher and slugger offered, "We're all close friends. We all have fun being around each other. It's hard for us not to have fun."[7] League President Rod Roberto agrees. Shortly after the team won the championship, he commented that, "These guys are so close that you can't have a party at someone's house without 12 kids coming over." Perhaps as important, the Park View parents and coaches didn't place inordinate emphasis on winning. In fact, early in the competition, the coaches gave the players a choice—just have fun or try to win the whole thing. The players' decision? Win the whole thing *and* have fun.[8]

The ability of the Park View kids to stay grounded comes from strong family and community support and the guidance of their Manager Oscar Castro, Coach Ric Ramirez, and Roberto. The trio's philosophy was to make sure their key messages, working hard and having fun, did not get lost in the run for the crown. They always kept the best interests of the players and their families in mind and kept the players loose but focused. As a result, the players were able to stay level-headed, even during the postchampionship hoopla that included appearances on *The Tonight Show*, rallies attended by tens of thousands of adoring fans, and a command performance at the White House.

It is easy to view Park View as invincible sluggers now, but the Blue Bombers' nickname was hard earned. At the beginning of its championship quest, the Park View team may have been perceived as the powerful Goliath of its own District 42. However, the team assumed the role of David in subsequent tournaments, facing formidable foes that were giants in their own right. It started with Rancho Santa Margarita Little League, the two-time Southern California State Champions as 10- and 11-year-olds.

Outside of Southern California were other teams with similar dreams. Representative Leagues from Hawaii, Texas, Georgia, and Chinese Taipei all considered themselves the "team to beat" in the 2009 road to Williamsport. The magical ride ended with a game against the representatives from Chinese Taipei, a region that had won the World Series Championship 17 times, that forced Park View to play a different brand of baseball. Park View's road was by no means smooth and many hurdles and obstacles were thrown in their path in the form of eight elimination games and accusations of doctored bats and false birth certificates. Park View overcame it all, and on August 30, 2009, they became the 63rd team to raise the Championship Flag in Williamsport. The journey of the Blue Bombers is instructional and inspirational, providing a road map for Little League players, coaches, and parents. This is their story.

A Dream Come True

> *"The one constant through all the years has been baseball. America has rolled by like an army of steamrollers. It has been erased like a blackboard, rebuilt, and erased again. But baseball has marked the time. This field, this game: it's a part of our past. It reminds us of all that once was good and it could be again. If you build it, people will come. People will most definitely come."*
>
> —From the motion picture *Field of Dreams*, 1989[1]

It was October 30, 2009, exactly 2 months after Park View Little League's amazing 6–3 victory over the international champion Chinese Taipei. The players were wearing their baby blue West uniforms as they gathered at the San Diego Hall of Champions Sports Museum to celebrate their recent Little League World Series Championship. League President Rod Roberto was set to lead the festivities with awards, team photos, and highlight films. Players dove into pizza, courtesy of actor and comedian George Lopez. Lopez, like many others, had seen the team play on national television. They had earned his admiration, and he wanted to reach out to congratulate them. We were here to meet with the players as part of our research for this book. ESPN and Channel 4 San Diego were also here interviewing the players as well, and we would be competing against them for the players' time.

Outside the Hall of Champions, the kids were playing around on the grass, acting like 12- and 13-year-olds, wearing the baby blue jerseys and hats they wore in Williamsport, Pennsylvania. Inside, past the famous San Diego Chicken replica and the huge silver rotating discus thrower, things were just getting started. Between coordinating the events for the evening and accommodating ESPN, Channel 4 San Diego, and us, Roberto had his hands full.

"Let's just set you up with a table, and we can put you over there where it's a little quiet. We're going to send people over to you one at a time."

We ended up in the section of the museum that houses several miscellaneous exhibits. Old hydroplanes rested awkwardly next to skateboarding exhibits and a spot dedicated to San Diego native Bill Walton and the San Diego Rockets of the early NBA days. Almost immediately, the first player, Oscar Castro, was sent over. Oscar's dad is the manager of the team. Usually we expect 12- and 13-year-old kids to be self-conscious or flustered by an interview, but then we remembered that they had been through this process countless times over the past 2 months. They were old pros. At the same time, Oscar seems to have retained his innocence, and his words were unguarded and fresh.

Oscar was the team's third baseman and relief pitcher. He has been playing baseball since he was 4 years old. He first played soccer, but after seeing his uncle Andrew, who is only 1 year older, play baseball, he told his dad he wanted to pick up a bat instead. He has been playing ever since. That's one of the hallmarks of this team. All of the kids love the game of baseball, and they have been playing it from a very early age.[2]

Luke Ramirez towered over us. Luke was a remarkable pitcher and power hitter who also spent time at first base. His father is Coach Ric Ramirez. Luke pitched Park View to two victories in the Little League World Series, including the United States clincher over the Southwest representative from Texas. He also slugged four massive home runs that soared over the 225-foot sign and into the grassy hillside of Lamade Stadium. After all of the attention he has received for those exploits, he continues to be humble. Through it all, although he had an idea that the team could win the Little League World Series, the thought was too abstract for him to comprehend.

"It seemed so impossible that we could win the championship. You can't wrap your head around it."[3]

Bradley Roberto is Park View League President Roberto's son and the right fielder. Bradley was one of the first players in the nucleus of what would become the Blue Bombers. He has been playing with Daniel "Junior" Porras, one of the team's catchers, since his first year of T-ball, and he has known fellow teammates Seth Godfrey and Bulla Graft almost since the beginning.

Bradley's biggest individual memory of the Series is when he hit a home run in the Great Lakes game that they won 15–0 to start off the series.

"Do you still have the ball?"

"It's at my house," he said with pride.[4] But that pride pales in comparison to when he talked about his teammates and the championship. You could tell that the team accomplishments were the most important thing to him, not individual honors.

Junior came by and offered a firm handshake. One of the team's two catchers, he started playing T-ball at the age of 3 and remembered not wanting to do anything but hit "squishy" balls thrown by his dad in the backyard. At some point, he graduated to hitting hard balls and "breaking a lot of windows."

Junior vividly recalled when the team arrived in Williamsport for the first time early in the morning, the Lamade Stadium lights blazing. Like countless other boys, he had watched the Little League World Series since he was very young. He always dreamed of the moment when thousands of people would be watching and the TV cameras would roll. When they won, he was in shock as he realized the Blue Bombers were "the best in the whole world."

"We felt like rock stars," and admitted that despite the help of coaches and parents, at times it was very hard to keep that fame in perspective.[5]

Seth Godfrey is the Bombers' third baseman. He too started playing baseball at the age of 4 and "pretty much fell in love with it." When we talked to his dad, Russell, later, he confirmed this, recalling "I never had to beg him to get ready for practice. He always looked forward to it." Seth has been playing with many of the other kids for a long time, and he echoed the importance of the camaraderie and brotherhood. He brought up the parties they've had at Andy Rios's house, seemingly the place to be.[6] Andy is the shortstop, and he lives in the same house where San Diego Padres and Major League baseball (MLB) All-Star Adrian Gonzalez grew up. Adrian has become a big fan of the team. The house has a pool and a batting cage that the kids take full advantage of whenever they have the chance.

Isaiah Armenta was the newcomer to the group. He only joined the team this year, at a very opportune time, when his family moved within the Park View boundaries. However, he has been playing against most of the Park View players for years as part of their earliest "archrival" South Bay Little League, and they all knew each other. Baseball was his favorite sport and the only one he has taken seriously. Isaiah has a very grown-up take on the experience. He feels the game builds character and prepares kids for life. He is also adamant that it is about the team, not the individuals. Isaiah was Park View's number-three starting pitcher and struck out 50 players during the tournament.[7]

The last of the players to be interviewed that evening was Markus Melin, the center fielder. We joked more about how Andy's house was the place to be. Then he offered an insightful reason for why he likes baseball so much.

"I love baseball because it always catches you by surprise. If you're not feeling good that day, it can pick you up."[8]

The parents and board members reinforced much of what we heard from the players but also provided new food for thought.

Luke Ramirez's mom, Kasey, was very proud of Luke, Ric, and the team. At the same time, she admitted that there was no rule book when it came to guiding the kids through something like this.

"Luke has been real humble, real good about it. It is easy to keep him grounded."[9]

Much of that comes from his upbringing, but it also comes from his makeup as a person. The same can be said for all of these kids.

When asked whether there was a time when they knew they would win the championship, she had an interesting answer.

"All of the stars had to align perfectly for this to even happen."[10]

Jim Conlin, father of Blue Bomber left fielder Nick, never pushed Nick to play any sport. Instead, he helped him figure out which sport he wanted to play and cultivated that interest. Jim has coached Nick from the beginning, only stepping aside over the past few years. He feels the key was to help the coaches behind the scenes and "do whatever it takes," confirming the important role the parents played in helping this team win the championship. That included throwing batting practice and staying out of the way of the coaches so they could execute their plan.

Beyond coaching, Jim taught Nick the game on a daily basis. They would talk in the car after a game, go over what Nick learned that day in practice, or just watch games together.

"We would talk about the little things to do to be successful—and stress fundamentals from the very beginning."[11]

Russell Godfrey, Seth's father, is another parent who did not push his kid into baseball. He was a helper coach, doing anything that needed to be done. He feels fortunate that Seth was one of the players chosen to join this team.

To Russell, one of the most important factors in the team's improvement was team chemistry that came with playing so many games together. In fact, at least eight of the players on the Park View team have played around 150 games during their 3 years together. That's like a full season in Major League baseball.[12] When they were not playing with each other, they were playing against each other, particularly during the regular Little League season. The team developed their core skills and their unique chemistry playing Little League games, including winter ball. To give them further experience and help them get past Rancho Santa Margarita, the team's nemesis from the 10- and 11-year-old seasons, the kids also played travel ball, seeking out the best teams, not just in San Diego, but in Orange County and Los Angeles. The teams they played were formed from the best players throughout the country, not just one zip code like Park View.

As the celebration was beginning to wind down, Cory and Pua, the parents of Bulla Graft, the team's second baseman, stopped by to share some of their thoughts.

Cory coached most of these kids with Rod Roberto until the 11-year-old season when they handed the reins over to Oscar Castro Sr. and Ric Ramirez. Bulla picked up his love of the game from his older brother, his best friend, and a great mentor of the game.

Bulla's parents believe that home life was an important key to the team chemistry, the stability, and support the parents gave their kids. They also credited the coaches with "treating every kid like their very own son." The coaches were the first ones to get the kids back on the path when they strayed and kept them focused on their goals. They also had an open-door policy with the parents and kept them in the loop on the decision process.[13]

Finally, one of the coaches had some time for an interview. Oscar Castro Sr. is the manager of the team. The Castros are a baseball family (and softball in the case of his niece). Oscar has been coaching Little League and travel ball for about 10 years. He has an old-school philosophy—hard work and more hard work. He also expects the players to do what he asks them to do.

When Oscar first saw the team, he saw a great deal of talent, but he also thought they had not been pushed hard enough. His first step was to implement a cardio program to get them in better shape and get rid of their baby fat.

"You could see those bellies, including my kid's."

He attributed part of their later success to their fitness. But more importantly, to win, the kids had to buy in to what the coaches were trying to do. First and foremost, that meant *playing unselfishly* as a team. The team was certainly able to hit home runs, but Oscar and Ric taught them to do what the team needed. If that meant laying down a bunt, that's what they should do. They also taught the kids that being a team is an attitude—you have to believe in it and live it.[14]

As the festivities broke up, we talked with Shelly Garcia, a board member who did not travel with the boys, staying home, instead, to raise money to support the team. She experienced firsthand the incredible reaction from the people of San Diego and was over-whelmed by the outpouring of love for the team.[15]

The celebration at the Hall of Champions came to an end. This was an ideal venue for the Blue Bombers' celebration. All of these kids have at one time or another visited this hallowed place, including the Breitbard Hall of Fame on the mezzanine that exhibits plaques of sports heroes with a connection to San Diego. You will see many famous names, such as Maureen "Little Mo" Connolly, the first woman tennis player to win all four Grand Slam tournaments in the same year. The Splendid Splinter Ted Williams, the MLB Hall of Famer and the last to hit over .400 (.406 to be exact). Archie Moore, an adopted San Diegan and light heavyweight boxing champion. Florence Chadwick. Mickey Wright. Gene Littler. Lance Alworth. Brian Sipe, a member of the first Little League World Series Champion from San Diego, La Mesa Northern (now Fletcher Hills Little League). Randy Jones. Dave Winfield. Ken Norton. The one and only Mr. Padre Tony Gwynn. And many more.

At the end, the Hall has reserved spaces for future San Diegans who will one day rise to greatness. On this night, one can't help but think that perhaps one of these Park View kids will someday grace one of those spots. Or perhaps they will have a plaque for the entire team, which would be even more fitting. But even if that never comes to pass, their victory is already greater than a spot in this Hall of Fame because they accomplished it as a team, a band of brothers who love each other and America's Favorite Pastime. No one can ever take that away from them.

2 | Meet the Blue Bombers

"I can't believe they pay us to play baseball—something we did for free as kids."

—The Detroit News (September 27, 1999)—attributed to Sparky Anderson, Hall-of-Fame Major League baseball manager[1]

We have heard the names of the Blue Bombers, but who are they? They play so well together, and their skills are so polished that it is sometimes easy to forget that they are comprised of 12 young boys. Now is the time to find out more about each of the individuals who make up this championship team.

Courtesy of Upper Deck

ANDRES "ANDY" AGUSTIN RIOS #6[2]

Ht: 5' 2" | Wt: 129 | Age: 13 | Bats: R | Throws: R |

2009 All-Star Batting Stats

G	ABs	PA	R	1B	2B	3B	HR	RBI	AVG	OB%
26	87	97	43	25	3	0	16	42	.506	.557

Birthday: July 15, 1996

Favorite Food: Orange Chicken

Favorite Movie: *Step Brothers*

Favorite MLB Player: Dustin Pedroia, Boston Red Sox

Favorite Color: Green

Type of Music on iPod: Hip hop

Favorite Video Game: Call of Duty: Modern Warfare 2

All-Star Highlights: Double play against Chinese Taipei, two home runs in one inning and game tying two-run home run against Georgia

Leading off the formidable Blue Bomber lineup was Andy Rios Jr. Andy was the Blue Bombers' amazing shortstop and was also one of the teams' relief pitchers. He started playing baseball when he was only 3 years old in "Hotshots" at the YMCA. In Andy's own words, "I just fell in love with the game." Andy played second base before moving to shortstop. He developed his game by learning from his mistakes, getting his footwork right, and focusing on the fundamentals in his hitting.

Besides the championship victory, one of Andy's favorite memories was when the team won the District 42 championship on his 13th birthday, July 15. In fact, they won district on his birthday 3 years in a row. This time, his sister was nice enough to make cupcakes—except the players didn't eat them. They just threw them at Andy.

Andy is quite versatile, playing football and basketball besides baseball. He is very good at all of those sports and is not sure which direction he may ultimately go. Andy wants to be remembered as a team leader and "Mr. Clutch." He wants the team to be remembered as a family and a team that never embarrassed itself or its opponents.

Courtesy of Upper Deck

ENRICO "KIKO" ANTONIO GARCIA #19[3]

Ht: 5' 6" | Wt: 142 | Age: 13 | Bats: R | Throws: R |

2009 All-Star Batting Stats

G	ABs	PA	R	1B	2B	3B	HR	RBI	AVG	OB%
26	77	91	44	16	6	0	23	53	.584	.637

Birthday: August 19, 1996

Favorite Food: Pasta

Favorite Movie: *The Blind Side*

Favorite MLB Player: Tony Gwynn Sr., San Diego Padres

Favorite Color: Blue

Type of Music on iPod: All types

Favorite Video Game: Call of Duty: Modern Warfare 2

All-Star Highlights: The entire experience—pitching, hitting and fielding in every game

Enrico Antonio Garcia has gone by the nickname "Kiko" all his life. He took the second spot in the lineup for the last two games of the World Series, but he was the cleanup hitter for the rest of the games, making great contact and hitting with tremendous power. He anchored the pitching staff along with Luke Ramirez and Isaiah Armenta, combining a great fastball with an even better curve. He also played center field when he was not on the mound.

According to the Show Web site, the travel ball team Kiko now plays with, "Kiko has always had a passion for baseball." Besides baseball, Kiko enjoys playing basketball. He also played club soccer for many years. On top of that, he is a straight-A student at school.

When he is not playing sports or doing his homework, Kiko loves to watch ESPN Sports Center, MLB Channel, and go to the movies with his friends. Kiko likes being in pressure situations, both at the plate and on the mound. He wants the team to be remembered as a team that worked hard and never gave up. And he wants to be remembered as a team player.

Courtesy of Upper Deck

LUKE CRUZ RAMIREZ #27[4]

Ht: 6' 0" | Wt: 212 | Age: 13 | Bats: R | Throws: R |

2009 All-Star Batting Stats

G	ABs	PA	R	1B	2B	3B	HR	RBI	AVG	OB%
26	65	94	42	16	2	0	17	45	.538	.670

Birthday: May 15, 1996

Favorite Food: Chorizo burrito

Favorite Movie: *The Hangover*

Favorite MLB Player: Adrian Gonzalez, San Diego Padres

Favorite Color: West Blue

Type of Music on iPod: Hip-hop and R&B

Favorite Video Game: Call of Duty: Modern Warfare 2

All-Star Highlights: Record-breaking home run against San Antonio and closing a one-hitter to send the Blue Bombers to the World Series Championship game

Luke is the son of Ric Ramirez, one of the coaches. He was the number-three hitter in the lineup. Along with Kiko and Isaiah, he anchored the Park View pitching staff with his fiery fastball. Luke held opponents to a .158 batting average while striking out one of every three batters he faced. When he was not pitching, he played first base. Since both of his parents are teachers, it makes sense that Luke works hard in school and enjoys learning. He is particularly fond of math and has thoughts of becoming an engineer in the future if baseball does not pan out.

Luke's least favorite part of the tournament was when he suffered a head concussion in a game. He wants to be remembered as the team leader on and off the field. After the win, Luke was thrilled that the Blue Bombers brought home a championship to Chula Vista and San Diego. With all of the great moments Luke had in the World Series, it is fitting that he feels the most pivotal point was in the Georgia win when teammate Andy Rios homered to tie the game. He ultimately wants the team to be remembered as a team with heart and a bright light in San Diego's sports history.

Courtesy of Upper Deck

BULLA GRAFT #20[5]

Ht: 5' 5" | Wt: 126 | Age: 12 | Bats: L | Throws: R |

2009 All-Star Batting Stats

G	ABs	PA	R	1B	2B	3B	HR	RBI	AVG	OB%
26	80	95	47	15	6	1	16	36	.475	.558

Birthday: January 18, 1997

Favorite Food: Fried rice with spam and eggs

Favorite Movie: *Remember the Titans*

Favorite MLB Player: Derek Jeter, New York Yankees

Favorite Color: Red

Type of Music on iPod: Rap

Favorite Video Game: Call of Duty: Modern Warfare 2

All-Star Highlights: Driving in the go-ahead run in the World Series Championship game against Chinese Taipei

Bulla Graft was the second hitter for most of the tourney, assuming the all-important cleanup spot in the lineup for the last two games of the World Series. He was the Blue Bombers' second baseman and another one of their power hitters. Like Luke, Bulla has been very humble about Park View's accomplishments. According to his parents, Bulla "hasn't watched one game on video. He is just the same kid. He has always been that type of kid. He doesn't like to be in the spotlight. He doesn't like to brag. He won't even bring it up unless we bring it up." At the same time, if someone wants an autograph, Bulla will drop everything and make sure they get it.

When Bulla wasn't playing baseball at Williamsport, he enjoyed the swimming pool and the arcade, much more so than the homework he and several teammates had because of year-round school. Bulla valued the whole Little League World Series experience because, in his own words, "I was able to meet different players from different states and countries and play in front of 20,000 to 30,000 fans on awesome fields." He believes the Blue Bombers won because "we knew each other like the back of our hands on the ball field." Bulla summed it all up by saying, "I love my coaches and teammates."

Courtesy of Upper Deck

BRADLEY ROBERTO #16[6]

Ht: 5' 0" | Wt: 133 | Age: 12 | Bats: L | Throws: L |

2009 All-Star Batting Stats

G	ABs	PA	R	1B	2B	3B	HR	RBI	AVG	OB%
26	74	82	24	18	5	1	5	17	.392	.451

Birthday: October 11, 1996

Favorite Food: Sushi

Favorite Movie: Too many to pick one

Favorite MLB Player: Adrian Gonzales, San Diego Padres

Favorite Color: Blue

Type of Music on iPod: Hip-hop, rap, reggae

Favorite Video Game: Call of Duty: Modern Warfare 2

All-Star Highlights: Home run against Nevada and diving catch against Texas

Bradley batted fifth in the Blue Bomber lineup. The son of League President Rod Roberto, Bradley owned right field for the Bombers and also took the mound on occasion. Bradley has been playing ball since he was 4 years old. He followed his older brother Austin who played at Park View and has a younger brother Cody who is on the way up. Although baseball is Bradley's love, he also plays football. He mostly plays offensive line, but also gets in a few plays as fullback.

Bradley described his experience in Williamsport as "unbelievably amazing." Besides his individual contributions, Bradley's best memory of Williamsport was "spending time and winning with 11 of my best friends." His least favorite part of the World Series was their loss to Texas. He believes the Blue Bombers were able to come back from losses like that and win because they "worked hard in practice and off-days and never gave up." He wants to be remembered as a base-ball player and a role model, and he wants the Blue Bombers to be remembered for the way they won the tournament—as a true team that respected the game.

Courtesy of Upper Deck

OSCAR RAUL CASTRO #24[7]

Ht: 5'5" | Wt: 144 | Age: 12 | Bats: R | Throws: R |

2009 All-Star Batting Stats

G	ABs	PA	R	1B	2B	3B	HR	RBI	AVG	OB%
26	55	64	22	17	2	1	5	20	.455	.531

Birthday: November 21, 1996

Favorite Food: Chorizo burritos and menudo

Favorite Movie: *Sandlot*

Favorite MLB Player: Jake Peavy, Chicago White Sox

Favorite Color: Blue

Type of Music on iPod: All types

Favorite Video Game: Call of Duty: Modern Warfare 2

All-Star Highlights: Hitting the grand slam home run against Rancho Santa Margarita to win the subdivisional tournament and making many double plays

Oscar Castro batted sixth for the World Series champions. He played numerous positions for the Blue Bombers. His favorite position was pitcher. Like many of his teammates, Oscar started playing ball at the age of 4, although he actually played soccer before that. One day, Oscar, his father, and his uncle Andrew saw a baseball game, and Oscar said he wanted to play baseball. They signed him up for T-ball and went from there. His dad coached him from the start. Oscar also plays Pop Warner football.

The entire Williamsport experience was the greatest time of young Oscar's life. He believes that Park View team will be remembered as a legendary team that broke the Little League home-run record. Oscar was very relaxed throughout the tournament and will always remember his funniest moment during the tournament— getting caught dancing in the dugout on television for millions to see. While there were many highs during the tournament, Oscar's least favorite moment was losing to Texas.

Courtesy of Upper Deck

DANIEL "JUNIOR" PORRAS JR. #7[8]

Ht: 5'0" | Wt: 118 | Age: 12 | Bats: R | Throws: R |

2009 All-Star Batting Stats

G	ABs	PA	R	1B	2B	3B	HR	RBI	AVG	OB%
26	53	57	11	8	1	0	2	12	.208	.246

Birthday: August 28, 1996

Favorite Food: Chili cheese hotdogs

Favorite Movie: *2012*

Favorite MLB Player: Joe Mauer, Minnesota Twins

Favorite Color: Yellow

Type of Music on iPod: Hip-hop and rap

Favorite Video Game: Call of Duty: Modern Warfare 2

All-Star Highlights: Hitting in the last inning of the Little League World Series game against Georgia and eventually winning that game at the very last minute

Daniel, "Junior" to his friends and family, was the number-seven hitter and the Bombers' ironman catcher. He started playing at the age of 3, but his love of the game did not take hold until he was around 10, when he finally knew it was the sport for him. That was when he really started to put his mind to learning the mental part of the game and improving his skills.

Junior and Andy Rios are charter members of the Park View team. Junior thinks Park View won "because most of us have been together since we were 6 or 7 years old and knew exactly what each other were thinking. It's instinctive." Junior remembers Williamsport as a very nerve-racking time. He was also not too fond of the hot weather and the flying bugs. However, the excitement and fun outweighed those challenges because of all of the quality time spent with his teammates and the chance to play for a world championship.

Junior wants to be remembered as "a player who never gave up and always hustled," and he wants the team to go down as "one of the greatest teams in history to win the Little League World Series."

Courtesy of Upper Deck

ISAIAH ARMENTA #23[9]

Ht: 5' 7" | Wt: 204 | Age: 12 | Bats: R | Throws: R |

2009 All-Star Batting Stats

G	ABs	PA	R	1B	2B	3B	HR	RBI	AVG	OB%
26	53	57	11	8	1	0	2	12	.208	.246

Birthday: January 4, 1997

Favorite Food: California burrito

Favorite Movie: *Avatar*

Favorite MLB Player: Too many to mention

Favorite Color: Blue

Type of Music on iPod: Hip-hop, R&B, *corrido, banda*

Favorite Video Game: Call of Duty: Modern Warfare 2

All-Star Highlights: Hitting a home run against Hawaii in the Western Region Tournament and starting the Little League World Series Championship game

Isaiah Armenta was one of three players who took the eighth spot in the lineup, along with Markus Melin and Nick Conlin. Nicknamed "the Bull" by his teammates, he has been playing baseball "basically my whole life." As with many of the other Blue Bombers, baseball is his favorite sport. However, unlike many of his teammates, he only plays baseball. Isaiah was the last piece of the team to fall into place, as he only joined them in late 2008 for the Gorillas' travel season. He came from South Bay, a rival of Park View, and knew all of the kids before he joined them. One of the most important lessons the coaches taught him was to be humble and do his talking on the field. They also convinced him to give "100 percent on every pitch."

Isaiah had a great time with his fellow Blue Bombers. When asked what he considered the funniest moment of the Little League World Series, he commented that there were too many to count, adding, "Imagine 12 teenage boys, and now imagine how many funny things they all say and do." He wants to be remembered as a team player who put the needs of his teammates over his own accomplishments. He also wants to be remembered as the best closer in Little League.

Courtesy of Upper Deck

MARKUS GREGORY MELIN #12[10]

Ht: 5' 2" | Wt: 90 | Age: 12 | Bats: R | Throws: R |

2009 All-Star Batting Stats

G	ABs	PA	R	1B	2B	3B	HR	RBI	AVG	OB%
25	21	27	3	1	2	0	0	2	.143	.333

Birthday: November 13, 1996

Favorite Food: Pepperoni pizza

Favorite Movie: *Underworld: Rise of the Lycans*

Favorite MLB Player: Manny Ramirez, L.A. Dodgers

Favorite Color: Blue

Type of Music on iPod: Rap and pop

Favorite Video Game: Call of Duty: Modern Warfare 2

All-Star Highlights: The diving catch against Georgia that resulted in a double play and made the #1 Web Gem on ESPN, beating out Tony Gwynn Jr.'s play

Markus Melin occupied the eighth slot in the lineup, mainly playing center field, but also pitching from time to time. Markus loves baseball because "it always catches you by surprise. If you are not feeling good that day, it can pick you up." Markus is very organized and always makes time for his homework and school, resulting in consistently good grades.

He got a thrill out of meeting players like San Diego Padre Tony Gwynn Jr. and Los Angeles Laker Kobe Bryant. He also found Williamsport to be an exciting experience, particularly the large crowds and meeting new kids from around the world. However, he found it stressful and exhausting with all the filming, appearances, practices, and games.

Besides the closeness of the team, Markus feels a big reason for the Blue Bombers' success was the great support from family and friends. Ultimately, he wants to be remembered as a player who never gave up and always gave 100 percent, whether he was healthy or sick.

Courtesy of Upper Deck

NICKOLAS CRUSE CONLIN #8[11]

Ht: 5' 1" | Wt: 123 | Age: 12 | Bats: R | Throws: R |

2009 All-Star Batting Stats

G	ABs	PA	R	1B	2B	3B	HR	RBI	AVG	OB%
26	19	27	6	4	1	0	0	1	.263	.481

Birthday: September 12, 1996

Favorite Food: Spam and rice

Favorite Movie: *The Longest Yard*

Favorite MLB Player: Tony Gwynn Jr., San Diego Padres

Favorite Color: Blue

Type of Music on iPod: Hip-hop and rap

Favorite Video Game: Call of Duty: Modern Warfare 2

All-Star Highlights: Scoring the winning run in the World Series U.S. semifinal game and hitting a double in the World Series Championship game

Nick was the third player who sometimes took the eighth position in the lineup. Nick plays all of the positions in the outfield. He has been part of the Park View team dating back to the formation of Team Soar after the 9-year-old season. Nick started playing organized baseball a little later than some of the others, at the age of 6. It is his favorite sport now, but he took his time coming to that conclusion, in part because his parents never pushed sports on him, wanting him to come to the decision naturally on his own.

Nick does not crave the limelight, and he does not look forward to interviews. He just likes to be around the other kids and play ball with them. Still, as part of the respect he has for his team and the sport, he fulfills his duties to appear with the family, sign autographs, and pay back the team's many fans. His favorite memory of the World Series was when the team mounted a come-from-behind victory against Chinese Taipei in the championship game *without* hitting any home runs. He enjoyed the Blue Bomber experience so much that his least favorite part of the championship run was sleeping because it got in the way of playing baseball and having fun with his teammates.

Courtesy of Upper Deck

SETH CHRISTOPHER GODFREY #13[12]

Ht: 5' 2" | Wt: 122 | Age: 12 | Bats: L | Throws: R |

2009 All-Star Batting Stats

G	ABs	PA	R	1B	2B	3B	HR	RBI	AVG	OB%
26	55	67	28	9	4	0	11	29	.436	.522

Birthday: July 12, 1996

Favorite Food: *Carne asada* fries

Favorite Movie: *The Blind Side*

Favorite MLB Player: Josh Hamilton, Texas Rangers

Favorite Color: Baby blue

Type of Music on iPod: Hip-hop and rap

Favorite Video Game: Major League Baseball 2K9

All-Star Highlights: Pitching the team to the divisional championship against Torrance and hitting two home runs

Seth Godfrey was the ninth hitter for the Blue Bombers and a strong third baseman, sometimes taking a turn at shortstop. He tried soccer and basketball, but from the age of 4, baseball has been his game. According to his father Russell, Seth "always had a passion for the game." He has been buddies with many of the other Park View players for a number of years.

Seth's biggest memory of Williamsport was getting to meet teams from all over the world who were all there for the same reason, to play baseball. He remembers one day when the team was eating lunch in the cafeteria and he saw the Mexico team laughing and having fun. The players went over to find out what they were doing. It turned out that the Mexico players were eating really spicy peppers, so Bradley asked if he could try one. He did, with predictable results—his mouth was on fire. Next, Luke decided to try half of one and the same thing happened. Both teams laughed long and hard and became friends.

Seth would ultimately like to be remembered as "the best number-nine hitter in the history of Little League baseball."

Courtesy of Upper Deck

JENSEN JEFFERY PETERSON #15[13]

Ht: 5' 3" | Wt: 143 | Age: 12 | Bats: R | Throws: R |

2009 All-Star Batting Stats

G	ABs	PA	R	1B	2B	3B	HR	RBI	AVG	OB%
26	26	29	8	5	0	0	3	4	.308	.379

Birthday: January 13, 1997

Favorite Food: Mexican

Favorite Movie: *Friday Night Lights*

Favorite MLB Player: Tony Gwynn Jr., San Diego Padres

Favorite Color: Blue

Type of Music on iPod: Rock

Favorite Video Game: Madden NFL 10

All-Star Highlights: Getting the hit that started the come-from-behind rally in the Championship game against Chinese Taipei

Jensen Peterson shared the catching duties with Junior, although he says his favorite position is third base. A baseball player since he was 5, Jensen also plays football. In fact, he is a middle linebacker, one of the tougher positions on the field. Unlike many of the other Blue Bombers, Jensen believes football is more his sport than baseball.

Jensen's funniest memory of Williamsport came when Coach Ramirez danced with the Little League mascot named "Dugout" in between innings at one of the games. Like many of his teammates, Jensen's least favorite part of the World Series was the loss to Texas, but he recalls many fond moments. For him, just "being able to be on the field and being able to play" was enough for him and the rest was a bonus. This comment reflects how humble Jensen is. When asked how he learned to be so humble and respectful, he answered, "My parents taught me well."

Jensen wants the team to be remembered as "a good-hearted team that worked very hard." In the end, he will remember the championship ride as a fun and incredible experience that he will never forget for the rest of his life.

3 | Destination Williamsport

"I won't be happy until we have every boy in America between the ages of six and sixteen wearing a glove and swinging a bat."

—Babe Ruth[1]

When you talk about the adolescent version of America's National Pastime, all roads lead to Little League, the granddaddy of all youth baseball leagues and it is still preeminent despite competition from Pony League, American Legion, and other forms of the sport. Little League wasn't the first to offer youth baseball, but it was the first to provide the opportunity to preteens in an organized way accessible to the masses. Its successful formula and approach have allowed it to endure and thrive.

The story of Little League baseball begins in Williamsport, Pennsylvania, in 1938. Carl Stotz is the acknowledged father of Little League, born of his desire to provide an organized form of baseball to his nephews. In that first year, Stotz experimented with different formats, equipment, and rules and didn't get around to staging any actual games. By 1939, he was sufficiently organized to put together the first season with three teams and the first board of directors that he christened operation "Little League."[2]

Stotz's initial goal in creating Little League was "to provide a wholesome program of baseball for the boys of Williamsport, as a way to teach them the ideals of sportsmanship, fair play, and teamwork."[3] The idea caught on slowly at first, mainly because of World War II, which ended May 7, 1945. At the end of 1945, there were 10 leagues and 600 players in Little League,[4] all in Pennsylvania. With the war over, the game started to take off. Little League added the first non-Pennsylvania league in 1947 in Hammonton, New Jersey, and held the first World Series, won by the Maynard Midgets of Williamsport.[5] By 1950, Little League had 306 leagues and over 18,000 players.[6]

The 1950s were a busy and exciting time for Little League. In 1953, CBS broadcasted the Little League World Series on television for the first time, with rookie announcer Jim McKay behind the mike.[7] There would be a 6-year gap before it made it back to television. Howard Cosell called the play-by-play for ABC radio, and Joey Jay became the first former Little Leaguer (from Middletown, Connecticut) to play Major League baseball when he signed with the Milwaukee Braves.[8] Many others would follow. There are 13 members of the Baseball Hall of Fame who played Little League baseball. Those 13 players, and the year of their induction, include: Wade Boggs (2005), George Brett (1999), Steve Carlton (1994), Gary Carter (2003), Rollie Fingers (1992), Jim "Catfish" Hunter (1987), Jim Palmer (1990), Nolan Ryan (1999), Mike Schmidt (1995), Tom Seaver (1992), Don Sutton (1998), Carl Yastrzemski (1989), and Robin Yount (1999).[9]

In 1955, Little League baseball found itself represented in all 48 United States.[10] By 1957, Little League had grown to 4,408 leagues and over 299,000 participants,[11] becoming truly international when Monterrey, Mexico, won the first of back-to-back titles.[12] Hollywood recently captured the 1957 Monterrey victory in a major motion picture titled *The Perfect Game*. In 1959, Little League passed the 5,000 league mark[13], and for the first time, hosted the World Series in its present location in South Williamsport, Pennsylvania.[14]

Little League's popularity continued to grow and each year yielded new achievements. Once again, the World Series final was broadcast live on ABC television in 1960 and returned in 1963 when ABC's Wide World of Sports televised the Little League World

Series Championship game for the first time.[15] It has been an annual summer event on ABC television since 1963. Some of the greatest broadcasters calling the play-by-play since 1963 have included Chris Schenkel, Mel Allen, Al Michaels, Curt Gowdy, Jim McKay, and Brent Musberger. ABC has also provided a Who's Who of color commentators, including Jackie Robinson, Ted Williams, Mickey Mantle, Bob Gibson, Carlton Fisk, Bob Uecker, Brooks Robinson, Don Drysdale, Willie Stargell, Jim Palmer, Johnny Bench, Tony Gwynn Sr., and Orel Hershiser.[16]

In 1964, the year Little League broke the 1,000,000 participant barrier for the first time,[17] the United States Congress granted a Charter of Federal Incorporation to Little League baseball.[18] In 1971, Howard J. Lamade Stadium, the main Little League World Series facility, expanded to 10,000 seats in addition to the grassy hillside that can hold another 30,000 fans.[19] The year 1982 saw the Kirkland, Washington, team beat Chinese Taipei, 6–0 in front of 40,000 fans.[20] Little League continued to grow steadily, topping 2 million participants in 1985 and reaching a high watermark of 2,591,190 in 1997.[21] It currently has nearly 200,000 teams and 2.3 million players participating in over 7,200 leagues in all 50 U.S. states and over 80 countries worldwide.[22] It continues to be immensely popular and the dream of millions of young baseball fans and players worldwide.

A team representing players from El Cajon and La Mesa, California, the La Mesa Northern All-Stars, became the first San Diego team to win the Little League World Series in 1961. Much has changed since that time, in Little League and in the world. In 1961, President John F. Kennedy led the United States and Russia built the Berlin Wall that would separate East and West Berlin for 28 years. In baseball, Roger Maris broke Babe Ruth's longstanding single-season home-run record by slugging 61 dingers, and National League baseball returned to New York in the form of the Mets, short for Metropolitans. Some things never change, as the New York Yankees defeated the Cincinnati Reds to win yet another World Series. In Little League baseball, total participants were still below 1,000,000 (896,000) and the sport had yet to become a televised international phenomenon.[23]

To get some perspective on how much Little League has changed and grown in the past 50 years, it is instructive to compare the experiences of the La Mesa and Park View teams. In the 1961 Little League World Series, the La Mesa team had to win three games in Williamsport to take the title, half the games Park View needed to win almost 50 years later.[24] In 2009, Park View played a total of 26 games, while the 1961 La Mesa team played a total of 13. La Mesa won the first two games, including one against defending champion Levittown, Pennsylvania, with walk-off home runs in extra innings. The championship game was also closely contested. In the bottom of the sixth inning, down 2–1, Michael Salvatore, also one of the pitching aces, cleared the fence with the walk-off winning three-run home run, putting the team over the top 4–2. The players went wild, mobbing each other and piling on. An estimated crowd of over 15,000 wildly cheered the boys.[25]

Over 5,000 fans greeted the 1961 La Mesa team when it returned home. The players received letters from various mayors and California Governor Earl Warren. In addition, the boys received special honors and extra attention from local schoolgirls. A local newspaper profiled each player, among them Brian Sipe, who told the reporter "he wanted to be a high school football quarterback." He went on to be a collegiate football star for San Diego State University and is in the school's Hall of Fame. Sipe also played for the NFL Cleveland Browns, where he won the league's MVP in 1980.[26]

"It's something you never forget," Chico Leonard, one of the La Mesa team's catchers, says. He still has the leather-bound scrapbook his mother gave him.[27]

"You don't realize how unique it is until you get older," says Rodger Cargin, the other team catcher. "The right people were in the right place at the right time."[28]

Sipe, the only 11-year-old on the team, calls the experience every little boy's dream.[29]

"It is unlike anything they'll do in their lives, and it will follow them the rest of their lives. It has for me and my friends that did it so many years ago."[30]

Despite some similarities, the La Mesa team and the Park View team played in very different worlds. Frank Foggiano, the only 10-year-old on the La Mesa team, found out that Little League rules prevented 10-year-old players from traveling with the team for the series, so he had to be replaced. He recalls that in those days, players didn't dream of making the major leagues, let alone playing high school or college ball. They were mainly out for fun. Foggiano did play high school ball and went on to the University of California San Diego, excelling in baseball and basketball. He even tried out with the San Diego Padres, but declined their offer. Foggiano couldn't make a living on the money they offered him. He had a wife and family to support.[31]

They had no travel teams in 1961. Equipment was scarce. Teams usually had one bat and a couple of balls. When they weren't playing in organized games, the kids would grab a field or a vacant lot and play "three flies up." All the bats were wood.[32] They would not become aluminum until 1971.[33] This resulted in fewer home runs, fewer runs scored, and more pitching duels, although the fences were closer. The players selected the All-Star team, not the coaches, who, as a rule, did less real instruction and more organizing of the team.

The circumstances in which the kids played back then differed significantly from today. They started playing the game later, at age 6 or 7, and played most of their games during summer vacation. Today's kids start T-ball at the age of 4 and many attend school year-round. In 1961, ABC did not regularly televise the Little League World Series. Annual coverage of the event wouldn't begin until 1963. The 1961 La Mesa team did not see the intense media scrutiny endured by Park View. ESPN did not exist (it debuted in 1979), and the team garnered only local attention and press coverage. One difference that may have played in Park View's favor was the double elimination tournament. If Little League still had single elimination tournaments, as they did in 1961, Park View would not have completed its magnificent run to the championship.

The current path to the Little League World Series is also different from 1961. In 1961, there were fewer tournaments. All-Star teams from individual leagues first participated at the district level, which comprises roughly 10 to 20 teams. There are over 650 districts worldwide. In larger states such as Pennsylvania, New York, Florida, and California, the district tournament winner advances to the sectional level. In smaller states, the district winner advances to the state or divisional tournament. The next step for some of the larger states is the subdivisional tournament, followed by the divisional tournament. The last hurdle before the Little League World Series is one of eight regional tournaments. Once a team makes it to the Williamsport Promised Land, it joins 15 other teams in a double-elimination tournament. With all of the differences between 1961 and 2009, one thing unites the La Mesa and Park View teams through time—their total passion and love for the game of baseball. In the bigger picture, Park View's championship, powered by a record-breaking 19 home runs in their six games played at Williamsport, coupled with the massive media coverage surrounding the team, will place them among the most elite champions in the annals of Little League history.

The Park View team hails from Chula Vista, California, the second-largest city in San Diego County[34] and the 14th largest in California.[35] The words *chula vista* are Spanish and can be roughly translated as "beautiful view" or the slang term "pretty little thing."[36] It is situated in the southern region of San Diego County near the international border with Mexico. Chula Vista is a fairly young community, with a median age of 33 years and over two-thirds of the population under the age of 46 years,[37] making it a great city for Little League and other youth sports.

From the 1880s until just before World War II, the area was mainly agricultural. Due to the climate and availability of water made possible by the Sweetwater Dam, citrus trees, particularly lemons, were the most successful crop. In fact, Chula Vista became the largest lemon-growing center in the world for a period of time.[38]

World War II brought significant and permanent change to the region, when Rohr Aircraft relocated to Chula Vista in early 1941. With the influx of workers and the demand for housing, the land once used for citrus groves disappeared, never to return. During and immediately after World War II, the population of Chula Vista tripled from 5,000 residents to 16,000.[39]

After the war, many of the factory workers and thousands of servicemen stayed in the area, resulting in a huge growth in population. During those years, numerous schools, homes, banks, restaurants, gas stations, and shopping centers opened to accommodate the growing number of residents. The last of the citrus groves and produce fields disappeared as Chula Vista became one of the largest communities in San Diego.[40]

Today, Chula Vista is largely a residential community. The largest employers are school districts, hospitals, and Rohr, which still retains a presence in the city. Its pleasant climate, strong sense of community, and family-friendly atmosphere make it a desirable place to live, and it appears the city will continue to expand in the future.[41]

Baseball has played a part in the Chula Vista community since the 1920s, when the city had a town team of its own.[42] Chula Vista has always been a strong supporter of the San Diego Padres, first as a minor-league member of the Pacific Coast League and then as a major-league franchise. It has a strong Little League presence with eight leagues in total, along with numerous Pony Leagues and travel teams.

The Park View league came into existence in 1969, a far cry from the league that it is today. Danny Vega coached in the Park View league from 1979 to 2002, and now he coaches varsity baseball at Otay Ranch High School in Chula Vista. His father also coached in the league and lent his support regularly.

Vega remembers back to the beginning, when there were only three Little League entries for the area, Chula Vista American, Chula Vista National, and Sweetwater Valley. Park View was the fledgling league and the "laughingstock," simply because they weren't very good. In the early years, Park View had teams in majors (11- and 12-year-olds), minors (9- and 10-year-olds) and caps (less than 9 years old). The majors had names from the major-league clubs—the Dodgers, Giants, Padres, Pirates, Astros, and Red Sox. The minor teams had names like Oilers and Vikings, and the caps were named after snakes, such as boas and sidewinders. Vega does not recall why they would have named teams after reptiles, but perhaps it has to do with the old saying that little boys love "snakes and snails and puppy dog tails."[43]

Vega started coaching the Park View minor-league Oilers in 1979 and continued through 1984, when he took a year off. Around that time, the league, down to only four major teams, nearly folded. Angie Edrozo, the president of the league at the time and Vega's sister, used to say to Danny, "I don't think this league is going to make it." In the nick of time, however, a group of about 20 core people lent their support to the league and nursed it through the lean years. Vega clearly recalls their names—Angie and her husband Bill, Walt and Robin Grady, Randy and Patty Byers, and many others. He is convinced that, if not for this dedicated group, Park View would not have had the chance to win the Little League World Series in 2009.[44]

During the tough times, from 1983 to 1985, the group did anything and everything to raise money for Park View—*carne asada* dinners, a Vegas trip, league dances at the American Legion hall. The kids used to hang around together outside while their parents danced inside the hall.[45]

"More than 25 years later, those kids still hang around together. They are lifetime friends, and that is rare. They all went through that together. In my opinion, that was the best time for Park View Little League. Because of the closeness, it was awesome. I was honored to be part of the league back then," Vega stated proudly.[46]

Through their efforts, the group made a difference and saved the league for the kids. As proof of the resilience of the league, in 1987, the senior team (ages 14 through 16) won the California State Championship, the first time a team from the league had won a championship of that magnitude. There was no World Series for the senior division at that time. Vega's brother-in-law Bill Edrozo managed that team. The championship had a big impact on Park View Little League. The seniors suddenly grew from two to six teams, the majors from four to eight, and the minors from four to six. Everyone wanted to be in the Park View league, much like today, although the impact of the 1987 victory did not approach the significance of the 2009 championship.[47]

But leagues fluctuate, mainly because the biggest supporters of the leagues are the parents, and when their children graduate from the league, the parents go with them. Most of the 20 or so stalwart parents left, with the exception of Vega, Edrozo, and a few others.[48] There were more tough years between 1989 and 1991, when Mike McNaughton got involved with the league.

McNaughton has played a role in the Park View league for about 18 years, initially as a coach. When he found himself complaining a little too much about the state of the league, he decided to do something about it and became a board member. On the board, he served in most capacities, including secretary, field maintenance, and most recently, equipment officer. He characterizes himself as a "behind-the-scenes president." He has never sought the official position because he doesn't care to "take the phone calls that go along with the job." McNaughton now coaches varsity baseball at Otay Ranch High School with Vega.[49]

McNaughton came into a struggling league in 1991. The financial strength of the league lagged largely due to demographics and per capita income in the Park View territory. As a result, the league had substandard fields, uniforms, and equipment. McNaughton's philosophy is that the better your field, equipment, and uniforms, the better you feel about your team, and the better you will play. In his words, "You are going to play as good as your surroundings. If you are in the best uniform on the best field with the best equipment, you are going to play the best baseball." Tired of bad equipment, he utilized his network built as an employee with a local mechanical contractor to obtain donations and upgrade everything for the league. Through the efforts of McNaughton, Vega, and other local supporters such as Rena Bospflug, Don and Karen Rhodes, and Alan Hayward, the league rebounded.[50]

Through the years, Park View has come to be regarded as one of the dominant leagues in the area, along with neighboring Eastlake and Sweetwater Valley Little Leagues. They have won more than their fair share of division and sectional titles, and there have been great years. In 1994, the 10-year-old team went to San Bernardino for the subdivisional tournament. In 1997, the 10-year-old junior and senior teams all brought home a championship flag. McNaughton had the good fortune to coach some very talented Junior League kids (ages 13 and 14) to three consecutive undefeated seasons with a combined record of 72–0. And there has been more ebb and flow. The late 1990s saw the dismantling of the league to support the new Eastlake entry. The number of players in the league went from 400 to 200 and hovered between 200 and 250 for quite a while. As it did in 1985 and 1991, the league ultimately rebounded, aided by the influx of new homes in the area.[51] According to Vega, you always see people come and go, but every 3 or 4 years, you see a major transition. Change and ups and downs are inevitable.[52]

The league has also seen some good ballplayers. Perhaps the most memorable is Todd Pratt, who played in the league in the late 1970s and early 1980s. He went on to play 14 years in the majors (from 1992 to 2006) as a backup catcher with the Phillies, Mets, Cubs, and Braves. His biggest moment came in the tenth inning of Game Four of the 1999 National League Division Series when he homered to put the Mets up three games to one against Arizona.[53]

Today, the Park View league is here because of the dedication of past and present supporters and is in its best shape ever because of the recent championship the kids brought home. It is already a fairly big league and will only get bigger because everyone in the world knows who Park View is and wants to play for Park View. The league will continue to add more teams and McNaughton ordered equipment for over 500 players for the 2010 season. The current Park View situation recalls the aftermath of the 1961 Little League World Series, when La Mesa Little League capitalized on the enthusiasm for the league and a number of generous donations to build a new field that now houses Fletcher Hills Little League. Corporate sponsors came out in droves to help build the new stadium, and kids from throughout La Mesa and El Cajon clamored for a chance to play for the league. A similar revolution is taking place in Park View.

The momentum of the 2009 Little League World Series success could help Park View build a legacy that will make instability a thing of the past, at least for the next generation. This is the sincere hope of Rod Roberto, the current league president. He envisions a league that is self-sufficient and can safely navigate the traditional ups and downs a league faces. That means building up a nest egg that will get them through the tough times without compromising the quality of the kids' experience, allowing them to buy equipment and supplies when they need it. Roberto also intends to lease the practice fields from the cash- and resource-poor City of Chula Vista so Park View has more control over the condition of the fields, add a batting cage, and ensure the fields are properly maintained.[54] It seems Park View has a running start toward achieving those objectives.

4 | A Winning Strategy, Chemistry, and a Little Luck

Forging a Championship Team

"Baseball is a game of inches."
—Branch Rickey, Hall of Fame Major League baseball executive[1]

The Blue Bombers begin and end with Rod Roberto and his singular vision.

Roberto is in his third year as president of the Park View Little League, but he has been involved with the league as a coach since 2001. Like many parents, his tenure with the league began when his son Bradley started playing T-ball at the ripe old age of 4.[2]

Roberto has coached youth baseball for 9 years, getting into it because of his son Bradley. He is a San Diego native with three boys, Austin, 14, Bradley, 13, and Cody, 8. All of them play baseball. Roberto played ball in Little League and Bonita Vista High School as an outfielder. As an adult, Roberto also played several years of travel softball in the United States Specialty Sports Association (USSSA). During that time, he met local legend Jim Tuyay, a long-time USSSA travel team and tournament organizer. Many of the USSSA teammates and opponents became good friends and keep in touch, especially since many of their children play baseball and other sports with and against each other.[3]

Roberto's strategy emerged over a period of years as he coached his son's teams. Bradley's T-ball teammate was Junior, who played catcher. The two were soon joined by Andy, and with a nucleus of three, formed the core middle positions of a potentially formidable team. All three players were proficient at catcher, pitcher, and short-stop. Other players came into the picture. When the kids were 8, Seth joined Bradley, Junior, and Andy, and together, they won Park View's Minor "A" championship. They also played winter ball with each other. At 9, Junior, Bradley, and Andy made the 10-year-old All-Stars, along with Markus and Bulla.[4]

When the boys were 10, Roberto coached the All-Star team with Cory Graft, father of Bulla, Park View's second baseman. All but two of the members of this team would ultimately make up the 12-year-old team, while Kiko and Isaiah would join them later. At this time, Roberto started to recognize that he had something special and his strategy began to crystallize. Two of the critical elements of this strategy involved improving the skills of the players and figuring out a way to keep them together.[5]

Enter travel ball. Roberto already had experience with travel teams from his USSSA days, and he understood how it worked. He understood that teams with budding talent needed to be challenged to continue to improve and grow. Little League, Pony League, and other youth baseball organizations typically have a well-defined season each year. Competition within each league is limited to a certain geographic area, and the caliber of the players is not always at the highest level. Travel ball is another form of organized youth baseball. There are no geographical limitations, so players from different towns, counties, cities, and states can theoretically play on the same team. Some teams pull the best talent from throughout the country to form superstar teams. The main format of travel ball is the tournament. Teams travel to various tournaments throughout the nation, pitting themselves against other teams that sometimes play as many games in a year as a major-league team might play.[6]

After the 8-year-old season, Roberto began to feel that Park View had some special players and wanted to see if those players would gel and improve with additional playing time against tougher opponents. He decided it was time to form a travel team to see what the kids could do. Reaching out to Mike Wanamaker of the neighboring South Bay Little League, he assembled a team of six Park View players and six South Bay players for one travel ball tournament—an experiment. The Park View kids were Andy, Bradley, Junior, Bulla, Markus, and Seth. After the tournament, Roberto decided to stock the travel ball team, now named Team Soar, with Park View players. Coaching with Cory Graft, he added Jensen, Nick, and Luke. Luke came into the picture because Roberto had met his father Ric about that time.[7]

Team Soar took its lumps early on, as the team only had local players from a couple of neighboring Little Leagues and competed against teams with more experienced players that were pulled from an entire county. Gradually, however, the players began to improve their skills, and the chemistry Roberto hoped would emerge began to show itself. That team chemistry not only developed for the players, but for the parents, something that would be crucial to the team's later success.[8] As Ramirez commented, referring to the relationship of players, parents, and coaches during the 2009 season, "There was no friction on this team with players or parents."[9]

After the 10-year-old season, in the summer of 2007, Oscar Castro Sr. entered the picture. His son had played on the 10-year-old All-Star team for Roberto. At that point, Castro and Roberto started to get to know each other and discussed how the kids could get together. Castro had his own travel ball team, the Gorillas, and Oscar and Kiko played on that team. Finally, after the 11-year-old season, Castro and Ramirez teamed up to run the Gorillas and packed the roster with Park View players, nine in all—Andy, Kiko, Luke, Isaiah, Bradley, Junior, Oscar, Bulla, and Seth. The team roster was complete with a rotating set of backups from other Chula Vista Little Leagues.[10]

According to Roberto, travel ball was critical to the development of the players, especially as they entered the 12-year-old season. Competition during the Little League regular season was not up to the level of the Park View team, and they did not always get the challenges they needed. Roberto realized after the 11-year-old All-Star season and the loss to Rancho Santa Margarita Little League, that the team needed to work hard on the mental part of their game. That included figuring out a way to beat tough opponents, concentrating every inning and every play, and having the fortitude to find a way to win when they were behind. Travel ball provided an environment to help the players accomplish that. Oddly enough, Little League regular season games also helped, because the kids learned to play with players of lesser talent and find ways to help those players contribute to the team, using whatever skills they possessed. Because errors tended to be more common in the regular season, it also helped the team's leaders learn how to rally players who made errors and get their heads back in the game.[11]

The travel ball strategy had a huge impact on the success of the team. In particular, it played a big part in Park View's ability to finally overcome Rancho Santa Margarita. Brent Rhylick, the Rancho Santa Margarita manager, agrees with this assessment.

"The difference between Park View and us was that we never played together as a travel ball team. There was football, basketball, and soccer, and when it was baseball season, we all came out and played baseball. If I had to do it over again, I probably would have pushed our league to focus on it a little better."[12]

The other prong to Roberto's strategy, keeping the kids together, presented more of a challenge. Several factors influenced his ability to meet this objective, including the selection of players for the All-Star team.

Park View allows the players to pick six All-Stars, the regular season coaches to pick four, and the All-Star coaches to pick the final two. Roberto ran the risk of some of his players not being selected. Fortunately, as early as the 10-year-old season, the eventual Blue Bombers had already emerged as the premier players of the league and their selection was virtually assured.[13]

The tradition of putting the best players on the 12-year-old All-Star team to give that team the best chance of reaching and winning the World Series created the other major obstacle to realizing

Roberto's dream. When the players were 11-year-olds, Roberto risked a number of his players being pulled up to the 12-year-old team because they were so exceptional. To avoid this, Roberto and the board of directors moved to establish an 11-year-old only All-Star team that would play independent of the traditional 11- and 12-year-old team. The vote for this change was close as many of the board members opposed the change.[14] In particular, McNaughton fought against the change from the beginning and held an overriding suspicion of Roberto's motives.

"When Rod came aboard as president, you could kind of see that he had an agenda to keep the 10-year-old team together. Little League is about the 12-year-old All-Star team. It's what we tell the kids from the day we start the regular season in February and March. Our goal is to get the best players on that All-Star team and get that All-Star team to the Little League World Series. Rod wanted to change the tradition because he knew some of the 11-year-olds would have been brought up to the 12-year-old team, and it would have split the karma, the bond that these guys had going."[15]

Roberto upset McNaughton by going in the face of Park View's tradition, which, he felt, was crucial to maintaining the integrity and quality of the 12-year-old All-Star team. However, after McNaughton saw the results of Roberto's plan, he changed his attitude.[16]

"As I saw the team build and do what it did, I became proud of what they had accomplished. When Roberto won in San Bernardino, when the last pitch was thrown, I sent him a text and said, 'I wanted you to know that you have my utmost respect for the way you engineered this team and did what you did.'"[17]

Ric and Kasey Ramirez also found themselves in an awkward situation. They were both on the board. Ramirez, a fellow coach and good friend of Roberto's for years, heartily supported the change. However, he noted that "it was a fight because it was something against the grain." His wife, Kasey, abstained because she saw both sides of the issues—she understood her husband's position, but she also understood the principle of putting the best kids on the 12-year-old team. The initiative passed—by *one* vote![18] Beyond this vote, Roberto believes the board was very important in realizing his vision. He worked closely with them and collaborated with them throughout the process. Without the board, Park View may have fallen short of their ultimate goal, and not just because of this one vote.[19]

The point of keeping the 11-year-olds together was to preserve the incredible team chemistry they had built up over the years.[20] It enabled them to handle the pressure associated with a run for the Little League World Series Championship and keep things in perspective. Bradley summed it up nicely. "You know you're doing your favorite thing with your best friends that you have known for a long time. It made it way easier."[21] All the other players echoed this thought that they were a group of close friends who picked each other up and had each other's backs. Knowing they had each other allowed them to take the pressure and turn it into something positive. The coaches recognized the awesome potential created by the team's chemistry and leveraged it for all it was worth. At the same time, they had a deep respect for it. As Coach Castro noted, "These guys trust each other and want to make a play for each other. If you love the guy that is on that mound, you are going to do everything you can to make that play. It is also picking each other up. If someone strikes out, you pick them up."[22]

Roberto's departure from the coaching ranks to become president left a void in the Park View All-Star dugout. Little League rules state that a league president cannot manage or coach a tournament team. Because of his past association with Roberto, Ramirez stepped up as his replacement. Since Castro's son had joined the league and he and Ramirez had worked with each other on the Gorillas, Castro was the logical choice to team up with Ramirez. So Ramirez took the manager slot vacated by Roberto, and Castro took the coaching position.[23]

By their own admission, Ramirez and Castro worked well together that first year, settling into a smooth working relationship. They found

:ason, however, that they needed to reverse their roles.
have been the manager, and Ramirez should have been
)m his years of travel ball, Castro had become effective
as the leadei and administrator. Ramirez, on the other hand, excelled
as the on-the-field guy and the teacher. So they switched roles for
the big season, and their partnership yielded a lasting benefit for the
team.[24, 25]

None of Roberto's strategy would have worked without support from the families of the players. Roberto always kept the parents
informed of his ideas and plans. He also emphasized the importance
of balance so the kids played other sports, like basketball and football.
They also spent enough time with their families and devoted themselves to their schoolwork. The parents responded to this approach
and were very supportive from the beginning.[26]

It is clear that Rod Roberto had an effective master plan and faithfully
executed it to great success. It helped that he also had two excellent
coaches and a talented group of ballplayers who loved the game and
played exceedingly well together. But mixed in with every success is a
little luck. A team can have all of the right ingredients for success, but
the stars also need to be aligned. Park View had all of those ingredients
in their 2009 season.

In past seasons, things had not gone as planned. Park View lost
to a very tough Rancho Santa Margarita team in the 2007 and 2008
subdivisional tournament. In those years, Rancho Santa Margarita
had luck on their side. All of their key players, including their pitchers, were healthy. They played all of their games at or near home,
avoiding the rigors of travel. They never drew the "extra" game, the
first-day game created by a five-team tournament, which would have
required them to play while the other teams in the tournament rested.
This would have also created back-to-back games for them, something that worries coaches because it sometimes creates a shortage
of available pitchers. On the other hand, Park View had to travel, a

trip compounded by the gridlock commonly found on Los Angeles freeways, and they drew the dreaded "extra" game.[27] Make no mistake. Rancho Santa Margarita had a good deal of talent and skill, but they played under close-to-ideal circumstances.

Park View had a little luck going for them too, even before the 2009 season. Their team got much stronger in 2008. The district boundaries were changed by the Little League district administrator before that season and Oscar, Kiko, and Coach Castro joined Park View.[28] Ramirez noted that after the 2007 season, Park View knew they needed to shore up their pitching, and the addition of Oscar and Kiko did just that.[29] Before the 2009 season, Park View also added Isaiah Armenta, who had moved within district boundaries, cementing a now deep pitching staff.[30]

The 2009 All-Star schedule aligned perfectly for Park View. They did not draw the "extra" games. They started by hosting the California District 42 Tournament on their home field. San Diego County hosted the four-team Section 7 Tournament, instead of Imperial County, and the subdivisional tournament as well. This meant Rancho Santa Margarita had to travel like Park View had in prior years. On top of that, Rancho Santa Margarita drew the "extra" game, and the schedule had them playing four games in a row. This time, injuries also plagued Rancho Santa Margarita. Their two top pitchers, Matthew Rhylick and Chris Reck, had injuries to their pitching arms and were unable to pitch. Rancho Santa Margarita even had to promote a nonroster player to shore up their pitching shortage. But everything seemed to fall into place for the Park View team in 2009.[31]

Even with that, the competition was close, just as it had been in the 2 previous years. In fact, Rancho Santa Margarita came within about 4 feet of victory. In the semifinal game in the winner's bracket, Luke took the mound for Park View. Rancho Santa Margarita, familiar with Luke from the 10- and 11-year-old All-Star tourneys, had some idea how to hit him. With the score tied 4–4 in the bottom of the sixth inning, Luke reached the pitch count limit of 85 pitches in a game. Isaiah, new to Park View and therefore Rancho Santa Margarita, came into the game to relieve him. The situation was tight, with a runner on second and two outs. The Rancho Santa Margarita hitter smacked a towering drive far over the outfield fence off Isaiah that was fortunately inches to the right of the right field foul pole. Isaiah went on to get the crucial out to end the inning. Tragedy averted, Park View went on to win 5–4 in seven innings.

If Park View had lost that game, they would have had to throw Kiko in the elimination game the next day, and he would not have been available for the championship game. Luke would not have been available either because of his pitch count.

The only notable exception to the good fortune Park View experienced in 2009 involved what could possibly have been one of the better players in Park View not on the All-Star team. His name was Javy Vega, a pitcher with a fastball comparable to Luke's, a curve to rival Kiko's, and as much power and hitting ability as anyone on the Park View team. Park View was familiar with Javy, as he had been one of the three non-Park View players on the Gorillas. In fact, it was Javy's team that had beat Coach Ramirez to win the regular season league championship.[32]

Coach Ramirez had this to say about Javy, "He's a little thicker than Kiko but about Kiko's size. And a righty, just a stud. With him, it would have been lights out. He would have been our fourth hitter and our number-one pitcher, on top of Luke and Kiko."[33] Park View had several players who could throw a 70-mile-per-hour fastball from Little League's 46-feet distance. That is comparable to a 90-mile-per-hour pitch from the major league 60½-feet distance. Most Little Leagues didn't have any players who throw with that velocity, but the Park View league had several players, including Vega.

Javy was the victim of a squabble in the South Bay between the Little League and Pony Leagues. Both leagues wanted him, and he and his father, José, were uncomfortable with the situation. Unfortunately, Javy did not live within the Park View boundaries. Ironically, he lived closer to the Park View field than any of the 12 Park View players. In fact, he could watch practice from his window. However, owing to the quirks of the boundaries, he was just outside of them.

"If his house could be moved a few more feet, he's in," according to Roberto. To preserve the integrity of the boundaries and ensure there was no question of the legitimacy of the Park View team, Roberto allowed Javy to play the regular season so he had a place to go, but made it clear that he would not be included on the 2009 All-Star team.[34] Roberto was just doing the right thing, but perhaps he had in mind the Danny Almonte scandal from the 2001 Little League World Series. Danny Almonte Rojas was a former Little League baseball pitcher who received extensive media coverage. With his awesome skills, he led the Bronx team, ironically nicknamed the "Baby Bombers" after the New York Yankees, to a third-place finish in the 2001 Little League World Series. With a high leg kick and a 76-mph fastball (the equivalent of a 103-mph major-league fastball),[35] the 5-foot-8 Almonte became a national sensation. On August 18, 2001, Almonte threw a perfect game, striking out the first 15 batters and 16 of the 18 he faced. The last perfect game was by Mexico's Angel Macias 44 years ago. However, weeks after the Little League World Series ended, it was revealed that he was 2 years too old to play Little League baseball. Almonte was retroactively declared ineligible, and the team was required to forfeit all their wins in the tournament play. Their records were also removed from the books, and they were required to demonstrate compliance with all regulations before they entered the 2002 tournament. Perhaps the worst disgrace was that his father, Felipe, was banned from Little League coaching or any other form of participation for life.[36] Ironically, a team from Oceanside, California, located at the opposite end of San Diego County from Park View, was beaten by Altamonte in the semifinal of the United States bracket. Park View would eventually face a team from Torrance, California, that had two pitchers who threw in the low 70s.

It is worth noting that throughout the 2009 season, the Park View organization never felt that a championship was inevitable, recognizing how important a part luck plays for any team. Quite the opposite. They knew that, despite the talent and ability of their players, they needed a little luck along the way, like Isaiah Armenta moving into the Park View league and Rancho Santa Margarita drawing the five-team bracket in the subdivisional tournament and having to play without a day's rest.[37] All of this talk of luck takes nothing away from the highly talented Blue Bombers and their magnificent run. In fact, Brent Rhylick, the manager of Rancho Santa Margarita, puts it best:

"The lineup that they had as 12-year-olds, nobody could touch them."[38]

5 | The Coaches

"Youngsters of Little League can survive undercoaching a lot better than overcoaching."

—Willie Mays[1]

The Little League Web site provides a detailed description of what it means to be a Little League coach. Coaches must be leaders and "recognize that they hold a position of trust and responsibility in a program that deals with a sensitive and formative period of a child's development." They must "have understanding, patience, and the capacity to work with children and inspire respect." Most importantly, coaches must realize that they are helping to shape the physical, mental, and emotional development of young people.[2]

The selection of the All-Star coaching staff was a very important step for Park View Little League. In order to be selected to manage or coach the team, the candidates must meet the eligibility requirements as specified by Little League in the Tournament Rules and Guidelines (in the *Official Regulations and Playing Rules Handbook*). The eligibility requirements for the majors division states that the manager and coach shall be regular season team managers and/or coaches from the majors division during the regular season. Coach Castro and Ramirez both met this requirement. Park View, like most Little Leagues, has the following base expectations for all managers and coaches, although they are not all-inclusive:

- Overall team leadership and accountability of parents, players, and fans.

- Teach and demonstrate good sportsmanship by respecting the rules, opponents, officials, teammates, and one's self.
- Encourage players at all times and will not damage the self-esteem of any player.
- Demonstrate that they have an appreciation of the philosophy of Little League.
- Attend all tournament mandatory coaching and safety clinics.
- Lead by example in shaping acceptable behavior patterns, whether the team wins or loses.
- Respect the judgment and the position of authority of the umpire.
- Responsible for understanding, complying with, and enforcing all local and national Little League rules, regulations, and policies.
- Game and practice preparations and related decisions.
- Team communication of rules, schedules, and tournament events.
- Maintaining the field before and after games and practices.
- Motivating and keeping the team loose during games.
- Refrain from the use of insulting, embarrassing, foul, or abusive language.
- Be a good role model.
- Have the understanding, patience, and the capacity to work with players in the age group.[3]

Besides these responsibilities, managers and coaches also have to deal with the intangibles, such as parents who do not believe their sons get enough playing time and parents who get angry during the games. These emotional aspects of the game may take even more talent and ability than the manager's and coach's on-the-field responsibilities.

As the manager and coach of Park View, Oscar Castro Sr. and Ric Ramirez effectively filled these responsibilities. But they did so much more in the process, teaching their young players life lessons and respect for others and nurturing their love of the game of baseball. The commitment, challenges, and sacrifices made by Castro and Ramirez were extraordinary. Trying to juggle work and family with a 2-month tournament takes an enormous amount of time.

As individuals, Castro and Ramirez were well qualified to coach the Park View team. Castro is a San Diego native. He grew up around the San Diego State University area and played Little League and Pony League baseball. Baseball was big on his mother's side of the family, especially with his uncle. He learned technique, strategy, and workout routines from his uncle, often playing with his cousins. Oscar began coaching a few years before little Oscar started playing T-ball and has coached all of his teams.

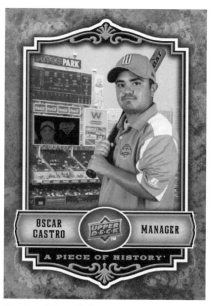 

Courtesy of Upper Deck   *Courtesy of Upper Deck*

This was Oscar's second year with the Park View All-Star team. Before that, he was at Eastlake, one of Park View's competitors. When Eastlake modified its boundaries to shed 150 of its 850 players and make the league more manageable, Oscar and son ended up in the Park View league. In the 11-year-old season, Oscar was the coach and

Ric was the manager. They switched roles in the 12-year-old season, to great effect.[4]

Ramirez also grew up in a baseball family and learned to love the game at an early age. His father played professional baseball in Mexico. While most of Ramirez's friends played soccer, he played baseball with his cousins.[5] Ramirez graduated in 1994 from the University of California San Diego, where he was the starting third baseman on a Tritons baseball team that went 33–8 and lost 5–1 to Wesleyan University in the D-III College World Series Championship Semifinals. A Chula Vista High School product, he led the team with six home runs that season, while batting .303 with 11 doubles, 24 runs, and 27 RBI.[6] He began coaching when his oldest son, Luke, began T-ball, and has been coaching Luke and his younger son, Ben, ever since.

Ramirez is a fifth-grade teacher at Myrtle S. Finney Elementary School. Being a teacher has helped him become a good coach, but coaching has also helped him become a better teacher. Respect, effort, and accountability play a role for both teachers and coaches. He works hard to teach his young players those qualities. Ramirez has learned much over the years about how to coach kids. When Luke was 10 years old, Ramirez stepped aside and obtained the services of outside coaches to help Luke with his hitting. Ramirez watched and learned as these coaches taught Luke and employed his newfound knowledge in his own coaching habits.[7]

Castro and Ramirez agree on the big picture when it comes to coaching. When it comes to tactics, philosophies, and personalities, they bring different elements to the table that combine to create an effective partnership. Castro calls himself "old school." He expects the kids to work hard and do what is asked of them, no questions asked. He firmly believes in the importance of the kids to understand and accept what he and Ric are trying to do. Team always comes first.[8]

As Castro exhorts, "If we ask you to bunt, bunt! They weren't used to it, because they can all hit home runs. It's an attitude. You can't just say it. You actually have to believe it."[9]

Castro is a big proponent of trust. He asks his players to stop a baseball with their chest if they need to. By doing that, the players develop trust in each other and want to make defensive plays for each other. Oscar truly believes that "if you love the guy that is on that mound, you are going to do everything defensively that you can to make that play." Offensively, "if someone strikes out, you pick them up." This was a big reason why the kids had such strong chemistry and friendship.[10]

Castro calls himself a disciplinarian. Although he tries to keep things loose, ultimately "I wanted them to know that I was not their friend, I am their coach—I'm here to teach and get them ready for the game." He sees himself as a bit of a father figure, but he admits that he "got on them a lot in the first year." They weren't used to that style—aggressiveness and honesty—and the lack of coddling, but they soon learned to flourish under it. For Oscar, it was critical that the kids commit to a disciplined approach and a singular focus.

Despite his self-professed toughness, the kids have a great deal of respect and love for Castro. Without exception, all of the players speak fondly of him, labeling him a father or an older brother, someone they really look up to.[11] Time and again, the players talk about their coaches and the critical role they played in winning the World Series Championship. Many talk about how their coaches kept them grounded when their pride started to get away from them. Others talk about how the coaches maintained their focus and consistently emphasized hard work. "They helped us when we would make mistakes. If we were down, Coach Castro and Coach Ramirez knew how to get us back up," acknowledged Jensen.[12] Shortstop extraordinaire Andy is very vocal about his coaches. "They made sure that we would always be respectful when we are at a game or out in public. They made sure that when we are talking to someone that we look them in the eyes out of respect."[13] Great coaching was obviously essential to this victory.

Another element of Castro's philosophy and approach is the development of a good relationship with the parents and the promotion of strong two-way communication. If the parents have any concerns, Castro's door is always open, and he makes sure they know it.[14]

"At the same time, my rule is that once we get going, don't talk to me about playing time or anything related to the games. I am the coach. I'm not trying to be mean. They understood that. At first, they may not have, but by the end, they knew how it worked. They always communicated positively with me."[15]

Trust is critical to the relationship with the parents as well. Castro tells the story of when the boys were staying in the dorms in San Bernardino during the Western Region Tournament. Castro and Ramirez had laid down the law with the players' moms. They could only see the kids for 10 minutes after the games. At first, the parents had visits with the kids on the off-days, but Castro and Ramirez soon realized that not all of the parents were able to travel and that some of the kids were not able to see their parents. On one of the off-days, Castro told the mothers who were traveling that they had to take "all" of the kids if they were going to go to the movie. The mothers made a decision to keep the kids together at the baseball complex.[16]

Perhaps the trust and confidence the parents had in Castro and Ramirez is best expressed by Bulla Graft's parents, Cory and Pua.

"While Oscar and Ric had the boys in their care, at least six or seven of them got sick and not one of us could even be allowed into the facility. When one gets sick, one coach babysits while the other coach takes the other kids to practice. One of the two coaches has to stay home and get him better, and that makes it harder for the other coach. My hat goes off to them because they took care of our boys for a month. They were separated from their families too. Away from their wives and away from their other children, and you know that is tough."[17]

Ric Ramirez buys into Castro's philosophy and approach, and he brings his own nuances to the field. Ramirez likes to focus the kids on certain themes, and he picks a new theme every year. When he teamed up with Castro for the 11-year-old season, he began to emphasize how important it was for the kids to love the game. He brought a focus on the mental part of the game, which he believes is 90 percent of a team's success. His theme for that season was the three Cs—courage, commitment, and consistency. After communicating the three Cs to the kids at the beginning of the season, he would remind them of it at every practice and before every game. His son, Luke, really took it to heart and inscribed each *C* on the underside of the bill of his cap. Ramirez's goal was to teach the kids more than just baseball. He wanted them to learn about life and retain lessons that would help them as they grew up.[18]

During the 12-year-old season, the theme was "RESPECT THE GAME." With this theme, he emphasized how important it was to give 100 percent all the time—between games, pitches, and innings and during every at bat and defensive play. By working hard and respecting themselves and their opponents, they were respecting the game. Beyond that, the players also learned to respect their parents and others. This respect for the game also focused on sportsmanship, which became the trademark for the Blue Bombers. After a win they would never show up the other team.[19]

Of course, kids are kids, and sometimes their excitement and enthusiasm can get the better of them. One such story involves the game where Park View finally beat Rancho Santa Margarita 5–4 in seven innings to win the subdivisional tournament and get to the divisional tournament against Torrance. The kids had focused heavily on how important it was to beat Rancho Santa Margarita. When they finally did it, they mobbed each other on the field as if they had won the World Series. Castro and Ramirez did not like this, not only because they still had a long way to go, but because it did not show respect for the other team and the game. They put a quick stop to their behavior, and it did not happen again. Coach Ramirez remembers vividly going over to the pile of elated players and telling them, "Quit acting like we're moving on. We haven't won anything yet, because you have to beat them again. Get off this field now."[20] At first, Brent Rhylick, one of the Rancho Santa Margarita coaches, was upset by this display. Later, upon reflection, he understood that Park View was not trying to show up Rancho Santa Margarita. They were merely ecstatic after overcoming their primary road block and nemesis.[21]

"You have to put yourself in their shoes. For the past 2 years, they have been trying to beat us. At the end of the day, they're just 12-year-old kids having fun."[22]

Castro and Ramirez harvested much fruit from the emphasis on the mental part of the game. The upshot was that the players always played for six innings, never letting up. A great illustration of this perseverance and focus came in Williamsport, Pennsylvania, during the United States semifinal game against the Georgia team. Down 10–5 after the top of the fourth inning, the Park View coaches reminded the team that "the game is six innings. Don't give up and finish strong. This is a strong team, and whoever is up in the sixth will come through." It's unusual for 12-year-olds to maintain this level of focus, but the players were not worried about the deficit and kept playing at 100 percent like they had been taught. They ultimately battled back to beat Georgia 11–10 in a dramatic fashion to move to the U.S. championship game.[23] This was just one of an amazing six games that the Blue Bombers won when they were on the brink of elimination, including two games in the Divisional Tournament against Torrance and three games in the Little League World Series. Another reason for their strong showing in elimination games may lie in something Junior said. When asked why the team did so well in elimination games, Junior stated emphatically, "Because we don't want to go home."[24] These guys loved playing with each other so much that they did not want the journey to end, the ultimate testament to their strong friendship.

Although the mental side of the game is critical, the physical side of the game, including conditioning and fundamentals, is also very important. From the time that Castro and Ramirez took charge of these players, their goal was to ensure the team never lost a game because they got tired or made an unforced error. Conditioning ensured the former did not happen and continuous drills took care of the latter. Although they enforced a conditioning routine from the beginning, the 2008 All-Star loss to Rancho Santa Margarita was their wake-up call.[25]

One of the main concerns was the team's hitting approach. They could certainly hit long home runs, and they won many games by "run ruling" their opponents, meaning they built a lead of 10 or more runs after four innings and the game was called. In essence, their very power became a weakness because they relied on their long ball game to compensate for potential weaknesses in other parts of their game. The coaches knew that the players needed to learn to be patient at the plate, wait for their pitch, and take what the pitcher was willing to give them.[26]

The coaches and players also worked hard together on the routine fundamentals of defense. Almost every practice was filled with drills rather than the typical coaching approach of taking ground balls and fly balls. Ramirez referred to this approach as "a bunch of miniclinics." One of Ramirez's favorite drills was "count 'em out." This drill involved reducing the fielding of a ground ball to its most basic components. When approaching a ground ball, the player would count out each component: 1–2 – Step – 3–4 – To the ball – 5–6 – Pick the ball up – 7–8 – Throw the ball – 9–10 – Follow through.[27]

This drill proved very helpful to Andy, the team's shortstop. The team was preparing to play in Lemon Grove for the Section 7 Tournament pitting the district All-Star champions against each other. Andy was struggling both with the drill and at the position and Coach Castro and Coach Ramirez were evaluating whether they should make a change, possibly moving Seth from third base to shortstop. The morning of the Lemon Grove game, Andy came to Coach Ramirez and asked if they could do the drill again. "After that day, I don't remember him making an error," Ramirez remarked proudly. His recollection was accurate. Andy nailed the drill, mastered the position, and never looked back, eventually making one of the more memorable plays of the Little League World Series, a play that was essential to Park View's victory of Chinese Taipei in the championship game.[28]

Though Coach Castro saw himself as the disciplinarian, with Coach Ramirez anchoring the teaching role, about halfway through the run to Williamsport, Ramirez volunteered to be the "bad guy." This was a big change for him, but he stepped into the role and had success with it. This gave Castro a break and cemented the respect the boys had for both men. They ultimately became a stronger coaching unit because of it.[29]

One of the ways the coaches kept the team focused was to limit their cell phone use and make sure they did their homework. This was not always popular with the players, but in retrospect, they all say that they appreciate the coaches' firmness. The coaches also helped them maintain their perspective, teaching them to work hard and, whatever else they did, always try to have fun. As Coach Castro always says, "It doesn't matter if you win or lose as long as you give your all."[30] One of the other messages the coaches relayed to the kids helped them in the aftermath of the championship, when they became full-blown celebrities. The coaches always told the players that playing baseball is a privilege, not to take it for granted, and be humble and thankful. Good advice.

Without a doubt, Castro and Ramirez were talented coaches who played a big part in bringing the trophy home to Park View and carrying it with pride and dignity. Still, they needed talented ballplayers to do it. They certainly had that.

6 | The District 42 Tournament

"The way a team plays as a whole determines its success. You may have the greatest bunch of individual stars in the world, but if they don't play together, the club won't be worth a dime."

—Babe Ruth[1]

They were not even a sure bet to win the District 42 Tournament, as they had never made it past that point before. In fact, Park View's dreams were nearly dashed during the first week of the tournament, when they met the team from Sweetwater Little League.

Rod Roberto, Oscar Castro Sr., and Ric Ramirez had laid the groundwork for Park View's big season. Most of the Park View team had played travel ball and All-Star ball together for 3 years, some longer. The team had developed strong chemistry and learned to pay attention to the mental side of the game. They had solidified their pitching staff and learned to be more patient at the plate. Now, it was time to begin their quest. The regular season was over, and the District 42 Tournament was about to begin.

On the first day that All-Star teams could practice, the Park View Little League Web site read "THE QUEST FOR WILLIAMSPORT BEGINS." Park View knew they had a team that could make a run at getting to the Little League World Series. They also knew that the competition in Southern California and all subsequent tournaments was going to be tough and that they needed to be near perfect if they were to represent the West at Williamsport.[2]

Before the tournament began, District 42 President Ernie Lucero had the responsibility of verifying that all players in the tournament met age and residence requirements.[3] That is, Little League requires that all players in the major division be 12 years old on April 30 of the season in which they are playing. They also have to live within the boundaries defined by their Little League.[4] Based on his review of the Park View players, Lucero found everything in order.[5] Despite his findings, rumors of age violations persisted throughout Park View's bid for the championship. This was particularly common in the case of Luke Ramirez because of his tremendous size (6-foot, 212 pounds).

Accusations about Luke being too old to play with the Park View team were common in conversation, in e-mails, and on blogs. Opposing players, who were typically much smaller than Luke, marveled at his size, mistaking him for a much-older player or even a coach. At the Little League World Series in the cafeteria, one of Park View's opponents saw Luke and commented, "Why is the coach wearing a uniform?" Fortunately, Luke is easy going and he let these comments roll off him. In fact, he is used to them by now. "I don't let it bother me." His mother Kasey was less accepting but has become more tolerant over the years. "It used to make me quite angry. I felt like people were calling us liars about his age and that used to frustrate me to no end. Since then, I've learned it comes with the territory."[6]

Standing 6 foot and weighing 212 pounds does make Ramirez a giant. Combining him with Isaiah at 5-foot-7, 204 pounds, and Kiko at 5-foot-6, 142 pounds, makes for an impressive and intimidating trio of players. Adding Bulla and Oscar, both at 5-foot-5, if based on size alone, the Park View team was the giant of the teams in the United States bracket in Williamsport. But questions could have been raised about Georgia's Cortez Broughton who came to Williamsport at 5-foot-11 and 226 pounds. If anyone should have been questioned about their age, it should have been Saudi Arabia's

Cameron Durley who was truly the giant of the tourney at 6-foot-2 and 233 pounds. And as a team, the Chinese Taipei squad had eight players taller than 5-foot-5, but their tallest player weighed in only at 140, which did not compare to the boys from Park View. While many questions were raised, all of these players met Little League's strict verification process.

Because of the Danny Almonte scandal in 2001, Little League revamped the age documentation rules, requiring leagues to provide original birth certificates instead of copies. In addition, the tournament director and league president were required to sign an affidavit confirming that the players' ages were verified. Taking no chances, Coach Ramirez gave Coach Castro Luke's original birth certificate. Coach Ramirez also carried a second original in his coaching bag and stashed a third original in his truck.[7]

Park View cohosted the District 42 Tournament with Luckie Waller Little League and was slated to host the championship game. The other participants included Chula Vista National, Southwest, Chula Vista American, South Bay, Sweetwater Valley, Eastlake, and Imperial Beach. The Park View team had won the 10-year-old and 11-year-old tournaments, so they were heavy favorites to take the District 42 title and move to the next level, the Section 7 Tournament.

Their first game on July 5 went as expected, a handy 16–0 victory over Luckie Waller. Park View's Kiko Garcia hit a first inning two-run bomb over the left-field fence to give them an early lead, something they would do often over the next 25 games. Kiko's home run was the first of a record-breaking 104 hit by the boys from Chula Vista. Kiko also sent an early message to opposing teams that Park View had some pretty effective pitching. He faced 13 batters and struck out 10 in a four-inning run-rule ending game. They followed that victory with another easy win over Imperial Beach (17–1) and clinched a tournament championship berth by easily handling Sweetwater 8–1 as Luke hit two long home runs on Park View's home field. In the first three games, Park View outscored their opponents 41–2, including 10 home runs.

They had a bit of a swagger going into the championship game and a rematch with Sweetwater. The boys from Park View were so confident that after their first win against Sweetwater they planned a victory celebration at the Rios house after the next game. Because every player has a cell phone, the players sent text messages that read *"Swim party at Andy's house after the game to celebrate our District championship."* The parents and coaches were not included on these text messages, but the party would eventually be cancelled after Sweetwater put a halt to their victory celebration.[8]

"The big 800-pound gorilla was present at the pretournament All-Star managers and coaches meeting" declared Sweetwater's manager Patrick Schneeman. He was referring to Park View's coaching duo of Ramirez and Castro. Schneeman knew Park View well. He was a member of Park View's 1978 All-Star team and grew up in Chula Vista. Patrick's son Daniel played travel ball with most of the Park View players and was one of a few kids outside of Park View Little League to be invited to play on their travel ball team—the Gorillas.[9]

The Sweetwater and Park View teams knew each other well as they were classmates and neighbors. The Sweetwater coaches and players all knew they needed to beat Park View if they were to advance. Despite this fact, Coach Schneeman only mentioned Park View once when he met with his players for their first All-Star practice. Instead of focusing on Park View or any of the other teams, he encouraged his players to focus on themselves, their team, and their goal to win the District 42 title. If they did that, the rest would take care of itself.[10]

Knowing most of the Park View players through travel ball, Schneeman felt they could play with them. "The only way to beat Park View is to outscore them," according to Coach Schneeman. Most teams tried throwing their off-speed pitchers knowing Park View would hit a fastball a mile. Coach Schneeman had a three-part formula for beating Park View. First, his team needed to get hits. Second, they needed to play error-free defense. Third, they needed some luck. Coach Schneeman felt that his team's pitching and defense equaled Park View's, so he focused primarily on hitting.[11]

Sweetwater had their ace pitcher Brandon Torio, a full-time Gorilla and travel ball teammate of some Park View players, going for them in the rematch with Park View, a must-win for them because they had come through the elimination bracket. Park View had ace pitcher Kiko on the mound, but in the end, Sweetwater pulled out a clutch 10–7 victory because they followed their coaches' formula. First and foremost, they hit, as Sweetwater scored 10 runs including a massive grand slam home run. They played error-free ball and watched as Park View made several uncharacteristic errors that led to a number of Sweetwater runs. Finally, everything went Sweetwater's way, illustrated by what happened in the bottom of the sixth inning. With one out and two runners on base, the hot-hitting Andy Rios came to the plate. Andy had already lined a home run over the center-field fence and was looking to even the score. On what looked like a run-scoring base hit, Sweetwater's shortstop Daniel Schneeman turned an amazing double play to give Sweetwater the incredible win over Park View and earn them another chance at the tournament championship. Sweetwater's celebration was loud and long. They had been looking forward to playing the role of spoiler all season and destroying Park View's dream. On this day, they took a giant step toward that goal and forced a cancellation of the swim party at the Rios household.

After the loss, Coaches Castro and Ramirez reflected on some tactical errors they made in the previous 8–1 win against Sweetwater. There are pitch count rules to protect young arms. Those rules can also affect strategy and can make the difference between winning and losing. For 11- and 12-year-olds, a pitcher may throw no more than 85 pitches in a game. There are also rules for how many days of rest a pitcher must have based on how many pitches he has thrown. If a player throws 61 or more pitches in a day, he must rest 3 calendar days. If a player throws 41–60 pitches in a day, he must rest 2 calendar days. If a player throws 21–40 pitches in a day, he must rest 1 calendar day.[12]

Luke had started that game. With the team up 8–1 late in the game, they pulled Luke, who had 72 pitches, and replaced him with

Isaiah. What was the tactical error the coaches made? Isaiah threw slightly more than 20 pitches, so neither he nor Luke was available for the rematch game with Sweetwater. When starting pitcher Kiko struggled, they went to their best available pitcher, Markus Melin, who on this day was unable to shut down the surging Sweetwater team. If the coaches had let Luke complete the 8–1 game, Isaiah would have been available in the next game and Park View might have been able to close out Sweetwater instead of facing an elimination game. It was a lesson they took to heart. Going forward, they always made sure they had two of their aces available if possible, watching the pitch count very closely.[13]

This first loss was not all bad for the Park View team. According to Coach Ramirez, it helped the kids realize that they were not invincible, even at the district level. It was also the first time the team realized how vulnerable it was to a good curveball. They needed to be able to handle the curve and be more selective at the plate if they were going to continue to advance. The coaches made sure to work on that, preaching patience to their young players and throwing them plenty of curveballs and off-speed pitches in batting practice.[14]

Going into the big game, the coaches also knew they needed to talk to the kids to pump up their confidence again. Coach Ramirez recalls, "The biggest message I remember giving the kids after the first loss was that it wasn't over; we still had a chance. This is what happens when you come into the game thinking you have it already won. That was the first of a couple of lessons that got us to the point of how we should look to an elimination game after a loss."[15]

Facing their first elimination game, Park View flamethrower Luke was available again and took the mound, but Sweetwater Little League was not overly concerned because they all had a decent idea how to hit Luke from travel ball and the game a few days earlier. With Luke walking the first two batters of the game, Coach Schneeman stayed with his hitting philosophy. Believing he needed to score first to keep the momentum from their previous win, he gave his number-three hitter the "green light" on the first pitch. Taking a walk was not part of this coach's strategy.[16] Fortunately for Park View, the strategy backfired. The batter hit into a double play and the rally ended. Luke won this early skirmish, and he buckled down to hold Sweetwater to only one run on a meager single over four and two-thirds innings. Pinch hitter Jensen Peterson blasted a long home run over the fence in left field in the fourth inning. But the drama came in the fifth inning, when Oscar blasted a grand slam home run and Coach Schneeman's dream of spoiling Park View's ride came to an end 8–2. Part of the difference was the adjustment the Park View coaches had made to ensure the Blue Bombers were more disciplined at the plate.

Putting his competitive spirit aside, Coach Schneeman instantly became a huge supporter of his neighbors and former Little League. "Although I wanted to spoil their dream, once they got by us, I was their biggest fan." In fact, he felt that his Sweetwater team helped Park View by beating them. He believes that this loss made them stronger because they faced adversity for the first time and rallied to overcome it. In the end, he felt he had a very talented team in Sweetwater and on any given day they could have beaten Park View. However, Schneeman believes the better team won.[17]

"As history will confirm, they are the best representatives in District 42. They got a lot farther than Sweetwater Valley would have."[18]

The Section 7 and Subdivisional Tournaments

"The riches of the game are in the thrills, not the money."
—Ernie Banks, Hall of Fame Chicago Cub[1]

After a wake-up call from neighboring Sweetwater Little League, the Green Machine from Park View (so named because of their white and green Park View uniforms and their precise dismantling of their opponents) traveled east 15 miles to the City of Lemon Grove, the host of the Section 7 Tournament. This tourney pitted four teams from the traditional baseball-rich south and east regions of San Diego and Imperial counties and was another double elimination tournament. The Park View team was ready to face the ace from each of these teams, who had aligned their pitching rotations so their top hurlers faced Park View.

Capturing even a sectional tournament flag is difficult for most Little League teams. But to capture the next four flags and win a place in the Little League World Series, Park View would have to prove it had a deep pitching staff and the mental and physical toughness to beat the best Southern California had to offer. Today, the Little League tournament is a difficult and lengthy journey. There are tournaments at the district, sectional, subdivisional, divisional, and regional levels before a team reaches the World Series.[2] The first four tournaments are double elimination.[3] This means if a team loses two games, it is eliminated. The regional and World Series tournaments are based on pool play, meaning that each team plays a certain number of games in a pool format. The top two teams from Pool A and Pool B advance to a single elimination format.[4]

The lowest common denominator is the district—California has about 70. Teams that win their district move to one of 16 sectional tournaments, six in Northern California[5] and 10 in Southern California.[6] The next level for Southern California teams is the subdivisional tournament, of which there are two, one for the northern

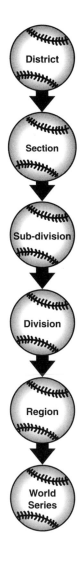

region and one for the southern region. The winner of each of these regions goes to the divisional tournament.[7] In Northern California, no subdivisional tournament is necessary and the region only holds a divisional tournament.[8] The winner of the divisional tournament goes to the West Region Tournament, with representatives from Arizona, Hawaii, Nevada, Northern California, Southern California, and Utah.[9] In all, there are eight regions representing the United States in World Series play at Williamsport.[10]

Entering the Section 7 Tournament, Park View had a long way to go. In the first game on July 18, the Imperial County representative from the City of Brawley, California, made Park View work for their 8–5 win. Park View started the game with what would become a common theme throughout the rest of their championship run— they scored early and often against the opponent. Leadoff hitter Bulla Graft opened with a double to right field. Andy Rios singled to center field, and big Luke hit a towering home run over the center-field fence to give Park View a quick 3–0 lead. The number-four starter for the Green Machine, Oscar, pitched three innings before giving the ball to Kiko to close out the game. Park View hit four more home runs in the game, including two solo shots from Garcia, a solo blast by Bulla, and a two-run homer from number-nine hitter, Seth.

In the second game, Park View easily handled Rancho San Diego Little League 9–1. Luke pitched a two-hitter over the first five innings and Park View added three more long balls to its record performance—one each from Garcia, Graft, and catcher Junior. With two wins under their belt, Park View was assured of playing in the Section 7 title game. In this game, they drew the host squad from Lemon Grove, California, winning another close game 5–3 to grab their second flag and advance to the subdivisional tournament. Starting pitcher Isaiah threw five and one-third innings of four-hit baseball. Unfortunately, two of those hits were solo home runs. Park View bats were unusually silent during this game, but they demonstrated the character of a championship team by making the most of every opportunity, scoring five runs on just five hits. True to form, they blasted three more home runs in this championship game, the final a two-run shot from Andy in the sixth inning to seal the victory. The Green Machine launched 11 home runs in the three Section 7 games. Although all of the games were competitive, Park View's opponents lacked the pitching depth that made Park View so strong. This was especially evident when those teams faced the powerful top half of the Park View lineup—Rios, Garcia, Graft, and Ramirez.

In the subdivisional tournament, Park View would ultimately face its toughest competition, the team that had eliminated it the previous 2 years, the two-time Southern California State champion team from Rancho Santa Margarita, California. However, this year, Park View was older, wiser, and better prepared. Into the bargain, Rancho Santa Margarita was playing on the road, as the tournament was hosted by a San Diego County team—the Clairemont Hilltoppers from District 32, just over 20 miles from the Park View field. Rancho Santa Margarita was also slated for the five-team bracket, requiring it to play games on consecutive days while Park View got a day of rest between games.

Catcher Junior Porras touched on another reason why Park View was finally ready to beat Rancho Santa Margarita. After the 11-year-old season, all the boys knew that they had to beat that team to have any chance to realize their dream. Rancho Santa Margarita became a rallying point for Junior and his teammates, motivating them to work extra hard and prompting the coaches to revise their strategy, focusing on doing the right things and executing the fundamentals. Junior believed the Green Machine was ready for this team in 2009.[11]

Like Park View, Rancho Santa Margarita did not have a cake walk in the Section 10 Tournament, losing to a tough Laguna Hills team 10–5 early in the tournament. It was a rude awakening for the team that had won the Southern California Division Championship 2 years running. They ultimately avenged that loss, winning three elimination games to advance, including two victories (11–1 and 12–4) over the same Laguna Hills team that had previously beat them. However,

Rancho Santa Margarita Manager Brent Rhylick had concerns about his team from the outset, chiefly because his pitching staff was not at full strength. In fact, his two best pitchers, his son Matthew and Chris Reck, had arm injuries sustained in previous games, a situation that would come back to haunt him as his team continued to progress.[12]

Little League baseball has been the leader in recognizing the rise in elbow and shoulder injuries and has taken dramatic steps to make baseball safe for its young players. In 2006, Little League implemented a pitch count, limiting the number of pitches a player can throw each game and dictating a required amount of rest between outings.[13] These pitch counts are for Little League game-quality pitches. However, the number of pitches thrown in game warm-ups or in practices are not typically counted. Many Little League pitchers, including the 12 Park View players, play on multiple teams during a season, and coaches rarely combine the number of pitches thrown on the various teams to calculate a total pitch count. With no official monitoring process between leagues, overthrowing is a real possibility unless coaches and parents stay on top of it. This issue can even affect as conscientious a coach as Brent Rhylick.

Despite Coach Rhylick's concerns, Rancho Santa Margarita started the tournament strong, besting Upland Foothill 20–3. Park View also won their first game over Corona National 14–4, during which they pounded out 13 hits, three over the center-field fence. This set up the much-anticipated rematch between Park View and Rancho Santa Margarita.

What was Coach Castro and Coach Ramirez's plan going into this crucial game? The Rancho Santa Margarita team had not changed significantly since Park View had seen them the previous year. Castro and Ramirez knew who their big hitters were and that they feasted on balls pitched on the outside of the plate, as most kids this age do. That meant Park View would try to throw a large number of pitches on the inside of the plate.[14]

Because Park View saw this as a huge game, the kids were very tense beforehand. Castro and Ramirez were totally focused, and it was their job to keep the kids focused. They knew that once the players hit the field, they would kick into their routine because they had practiced so hard and the fundamentals were ingrained in them.[15] According to Coach Ramirez, "Obviously, we knew what kind of a team they were, but I was confident that we could beat them."[16] The Park View 10-year-old All-Star team in 2007 did not resemble the 2010 squad as Andy, Kiko, and Isaiah were not on the 2007 roster. Andy missed All-Stars that year because he was on a father-and-son baseball trip to the East Coast that included 14 stadiums and a visit to Cooperstown. Kiko and Isaiah were both playing for another Little League.

On July 27, the two rivals faced off. From the outset, starting pitcher Luke had trouble finding the strike zone. In his four innings pitched he threw 85 pitches, hit one batter, threw one wild pitch, and walked four. This was not part of the script drafted by the coaches. Despite his wildness, Luke only gave up two runs on two hits, including a solo home run to lead off the fourth inning. Isaiah took the mound to start the fifth inning, only to be let down by his defense. A costly error by Bulla at second base contributed to Rancho Santa Margarita scoring the tying run. Both teams had a difficult time offensively. After six innings of regulation play, the score was deadlocked at 3–3. The two teams had only been able to produce a total of seven hits. The Green Machine accounted for five of those seven hits, including a two-run home run that Luke parked over the left-field fence.

In the top of the seventh, Park View finally made some noise. After a pep talk from Coach Castro, the boys scraped out two runs on only two hits. In the bottom half of the seventh, the first pitch from Isaiah resulted in a bobbled routine ground ball by Park View and allowed Rancho's leadoff hitter to reach first base. A passed ball and a single brought Rancho Santa Margarita to within one run. After only three pitches, Rancho Santa Margarita had served notice that they would not quit. Would Park View once again fold under pressure from their nemesis? Coach Castro calmly walked out to the mound to calm down his pitcher and talk defensive strategy with his players. The pep talk worked. Isaiah struck out the next batter, Rancho's number-three hitter, on three pitches. A ground ball fielder's choice by Rancho's cleanup hitter Matthew Rhylick on the very next pitch put the Green Machine one out closer to victory. Isaiah needed just five pitches to strike out the last batter. In a hard-fought game, Park View prevailed 5–4, finally besting Rancho Santa Margarita and earning a spot in the championship game.

There were many reasons why Park View was finally able to beat Rancho Santa Margarita. Among them, Coach Ramirez believes the kids executed the inside pitch strategy the coaches put into play and that the kids had also matured and played many innings with each other over the past year, improving their teamwork.[17]

After a 7–4 victory against Mission Trails, Rancho Santa Margarita prepared for a rematch with Park View. Unfortunately for Rancho Santa Margarita, they had nothing left in the tank and the championship game was a nonevent, Park View winning 16–1 and capturing their third title flag. The top five hitters for the Green Machine each homered, with the number-two hitter Bulla Graft smacking two bombs. Seth, Park View's dynamic number-nine hitter, also blasted a pair of home runs over the center-field fence. Park View hit a total of eight home runs in this championship game to put an exclamation point on the victory. In the end, ace pitcher Kiko struck out eight batters and gave up only four hits in his five and two-thirds innings.

Coach Rhylick knew his team had run out of gas after an awesome 3-year run.[18] "They were mentally and physically tired. I think we played something like 12 games in 14 days. And physically, the kids just couldn't do it."[19]

According to Rhylick, all of his players were very happy for the Park View team and watched every televised game, rooting for Park View to win it all. Ultimately, he gives Rod Roberto a lot of credit for planning ahead and putting together a winning strategy, the coaches for leading the players, and the kids for their execution and "God-given" talent.[20]

8 Mano a Mano

Squaring Off Against Torrance in the Divisional Tournament

"If you've ever been around a group of actors, you've noticed, no doubt, that they can talk of nothing else under the sun but acting. It's exactly the same way with baseball players."
—Christy Mathewson, Hall of Fame New York Giants pitcher[1]

In their first road trip, the Green Machine met Torrance Little League in the Southern California Divisional Championship Tournament hosted by Encino Little League. For this tournament, Park View drove 136 miles to Encino, north of Los Angeles, where their toughest challenge to date awaited. Park View's subdivisional triumph had boosted their confidence and cemented their belief in their ability to get to the Little League World Series. However, some say getting through the talented group of Southern California teams is the toughest part of earning the chance to play in Williamsport, and Park View still had to beat one more of those teams. Park View's previous foe, Rancho Santa Margarita coach Brent Rhylick, knew that Torrance was a solid team, having faced them in previous years.[2]

Rhylick commented, "Because we played Torrance in the finals as 10-year-olds, we knew that they were good. After Park View beat us, some of the coaches and I talked, and we thought it was going to be really interesting to see how Park View would play Torrance after being so emotionally drained after beating us."[3]

Torrance Little League felt pretty confident after getting through their sectional and subdivisional play. To this point, they were undefeated in tournament play, and they were thrilled that the games were only 30 miles from their field, giving them the home-field advantage. Although no team from Torrance's district had made it to this point since San Pedro in 1989, Torrance Manager Manny Olloque Jr. had a strong group of sluggers and deep pitching. And he felt they were ready to move to the next level.

In game one, Torrance threw their best punch at Park View in the form of David Aros, a good left-handed pitcher who consistently threw off-speed pitches to keep the powerful Green Machine lineup off balance. Aros was not even one of Torrance's aces, but he had good stuff, and Park View had not faced many good off-speed hurlers. The Torrance pitcher was capable of throwing a nasty curveball and slider and a good changeup. Park View had gotten in the habit of slugging home runs off a steady diet of fastballs, hitting 12 in the subdivisional tournament. A different style of pitching was one way to stop the Green Machine. More importantly, by pitching Aros, Torrance would have their two right-handed aces ready and waiting for games two and three (if it came to that).

For this game, Park View started big Luke Ramirez, who had trouble finding the strike zone early. Two wild pitches, two passed balls, six walks, three hit batters, and two defensive errors all played against Park View. After falling behind early in the game, Coach Castro changed pitchers often to keep everyone below the pitch count, keeping his options open for the next game.[4] In total, five players took the mound for Park View, while Torrance's Aros pitched a brilliant game, keeping Park View in check for four innings. Along with great pitching, Torrance unleashed its offense, scoring in each inning with eight hits, three of them line-drive home runs over the ivy-covered fences. The top four hitters for Torrance reached base 12 times in 16 plate appearances. Those batters scored 10 runs and belted two of the three home runs. There was no drama in this game as the Park View batters struck out in eight of their 15-plate appearances. When it was finally over, the Park View Little League team was shut out for the first, and only, time in the tournament 18–0 in a four-inning run-rule affair. Uncharacteristically, Park View had only three total base runners and two hits in this game. It was also the only game to date that Park View failed to hit a home run.

Little did Torrance realize that Castro and Ramirez had a longer-term strategy, and once they fell behind in this game, they employed it to ensure Park View had a fighting chance in games two and three. Before this game, they became aware that the parents of the Rancho Santa Margarita team had a Facebook page and discussed game results and strategy right on the Web. Coach Castro and Coach Ramirez studied these exchanges and learned that in the game they had lost, Rancho Santa Margarita had decided to keep their best pitching out of the game after they fell behind so they could come back in the next game and put their aces on the mound. Castro and Ramirez thought that was a great strategy and when they fell behind early in the Torrance game, they put it into action. They pitched everyone but Kiko and Isaiah and made sure they were available for the next game.[5]

Most teams would have been shell-shocked by an 18–0 loss. "When they got absolutely smoked in the first game we all thought they were done, and that they didn't have the mental fortitude to come back," stated Patrick Schneeman, Sweetwater's coach.[6]

They couldn't have been more wrong. Even an 18–0 route could not dim Park View's spirits, forged over years of playing together and overcoming setbacks and obstacles. Castro and Ramirez felt that this was a big game for many reasons. Most important, after this loss, the coaches realized that the team needed to get away from relying on the long ball and get back to basics. And the kids, who had been riding high, were once again willing to listen to their leaders. In response to such a challenge, most teams would take hacks at the batting cage, but Castro and Ramirez had a better idea—a game of Wiffle ball.[7]

Coach Ramirez, who usually threw batting practice, had thrown a lot of batting practice to the Green Machine during the first 11 games prior to Encino. With all of those pitches, his arm started to hurt around the time they started playing Torrance. This was in part because he was throwing a lot of the off-speed pitches that he and

Castro knew the kids were going to see as they advanced in the tournament. Wiffle balls gave Ramirez's aching arm a break and provided a way for the kids to focus on the ball again and get back a smooth, line-drive stroke. So the night of the Torrance defeat, the kids joined with their coaches and parents and played a game of Wiffle ball. By the time they were done, not only had they regrooved their swings, but they had let off some steam, had some fun, and were able to let go of the big loss.[8] In the end, Ramirez's sore arm played a big part in their championship run. Park View went on to blast 56 more home runs over their final 12 games en route to the championship.

This latest fine-tuning of Park View's hitting was part of an ongoing improvement program requiring that the kids sharpen their mental focus and continue to cultivate patience at the plate. In the District 42 Tournament, Coach Ramirez had the kids taking a hack at first pitches because the opposing pitchers did not typically have the well-developed curveball that later opponents threw. Gradually, the pitching got tougher and the curveball began to challenge Park View. This culminated in the first game against Torrance. After that game, Ramirez had them take the curveball early in the count, and they continued that strategy through the rest of their games. The kids became incredibly patient as a result, to the point that other coaches would approach Coach Ramirez and ask, "How are your kids so patient?" Taking pitches also had another benefit—the opposing pitcher threw more pitches and often had to be taken out earlier. Although the strategy sometimes backfired because good hitters would miss the chance to hit a fastball up the middle, it usually worked like a charm.[9]

From their point of view, Torrance had a reasonably clear view to the West Region Tournament and possibly Williamsport. Torrance Coach Manny Olloque felt that by saving their aces, who threw consistently in the low 70s, they would be able to dominate Park View and win the tournament.[10] This strategy eventually backfired as offense, rather than pitching and defense, dominated the final two games, especially the deciding third game. "If you are in a slugfest against Parkview, you are going to lose," according to Sweetwater Manager Schneeman.[11]

Park View also got some unintentional motivation from their opponent. In a postgame interview, Torrance's Coach Olloque made the comment, "Not to be overly confident, but Park View used five pitchers today, and we hit them all pretty well. If we play like we have been, everything should work out."[12] The Torrance parents were also overconfident after the 18–0 thumping of Park View. They were beginning to make plans for playing Utah at the West Region Tournament in San Bernardino, California, in a few days. In fact, Park View fans overheard Torrance parents say, "I can't believe Park View made it this far; they are bad!" The Green Machine heard about these comments, and it gave them additional motivation to come back.[13]

In the first of those two games, Park View came back to scrape out a 7–6 win, another close call in an elimination game for the team from Chula Vista. Luke hit a two-run home run over the right-field fence in the third inning. In the fifth inning with the game tied 3–3, the Green Machine's Kiko Garcia hit a grand slam off a 3–2 pitch. Torrance battled back in the bottom of the fourth with a couple of home runs of their own to narrow the lead to 7–6. They threatened again in the sixth inning, getting two two-out singles before Kiko struck out their number-three hitter Budrovich on four pitches.

"Today, a couple of mistakes were game changers, and we had to climb out of a hole," Torrance Coach Olloque said. Still, he felt confident as he prepared for the third game with his powerful hitters and a number of strong pitchers available.[14]

With a trip to the West Region Tournament at stake, the two teams squared off for the biggest game of their young careers. Getting to game three in Encino had given Park View some much-needed confidence. However, they did not have their top three starting pitchers, Kiko, Luke, or Isaiah, available, while Torrance did. Park View went with Oscar Castro as their starter, but pitching took a backseat to hitting in this game.

It started off well enough for Torrance as they got up 6–0 in the bottom of the first. Their awesome hitting earned them the nickname "The Big Red Machine" after hitting 33 homers in a 14–game stretch and averaging almost 10 runs per game. The lead did not last long as

Park View came right back with an eight-run top of the second, including a two-run homer by Roberto. That was followed shortly by a grand slam home run by Andy Rios on a 3–1 pitch to put Park View up by two after two innings. The Green Machine sent 12 batters to the plate and pounded out eight hits in the inning.

After little more than an inning, the teams had scored more runs than in the entire second game. After more of the same in the third inning, including a two-run homer to center field by Seth, the two teams were tied at 12 runs apiece.

After the game, Coach Olloque commented, "There was a lot of offense. You figure if you score 12 runs, you'd win the game. Yet, I knew it was going to be a slugfest."[15]

Park View put an exclamation point on the slugfest by scoring seven runs in the top of the fourth inning. The hot-hitting Seth banged his second long ball of the game, this time a game-winning grand slam. Three batters later, Luke hit a "no-doubt" two-run homer to quash any comeback hopes for Torrance. Leading 19–12, Park View brought in shortstop Andy Rios to close out the game and help nab their fourth tournament flag. In the end, it was a true team effort as three nonstarters pitched, and all 12 players scored.

"It's a little hard to swallow," Torrance Coach Olloque said. "I took my son to San Bernardino last season, and I thought, 'Why couldn't that be us?' It was a good run, but to get this close, it's tough."[16] Olloque did send a gracious e-mail to President Roberto congratulating Park View and urging them to keep winning.[17]

Park View was on its way to the West Region Tournament. Despite doing an exemplary job of rallying the kids from the crushing game one loss, the Park View coaches were not in perfect harmony up to this point. They had some disagreements about waving a runner home only to be thrown out or calling a bad pitch that was spanked over the fence. Sometimes they even second-guessed one another or changed strategy midcourse. There was one particular situation Coach Ramirez laughingly recalls that sums up their challenges.

"We were playing Torrance in the title game, and we knew it was going to be a slugfest. As we were sitting in the dugout, Seth was up on the mound throwing his curveball and his fastball and they were hitting him hard and scoring runs. But we were also scoring runs to keep things close. I looked at Coach Oscar and said we need to stop them with pitching. He stared at me with this blank look on his face. Then he shouted, 'What do you want me to throw?' I stared back and said, 'Dude, I don't know. My job is to get them hitting, and we're doing that.'"[18] Despite these rough spots, their partnership would start to click on all cylinders when the team reached San Bernardino.

As a postscript, Coach Schneeman of Sweetwater Little League offered this viewpoint of Park View's accomplishment. "I became a fan of Park View not just because you want to be able to say that the team that knocked you out won the Little League World Series. I am a fan because I know those kids. The Torrance manager probably became a fan because if you are going to get knocked out, why not get knocked out by the guys who win it all? It makes you feel a little bit better about your team, although Torrance probably would have won it all if they got by Park View."[19]

After the victory, President Roberto received a letter from the board of directors of Park View's local rival, Eastlake Little League. Besides congratulating Park View, the letter noted, "how difficult it is to win a district flag," and that "to get to the Western Region Tournament in San Bernardino is an outstanding accomplishment." The board closed the letter by asking Roberto to "tell the players to enjoy what they have accomplished and good luck!"[20]

9 | One Step Away
The West Region Tournament

"Boys, baseball is a game where you gotta have fun. You do that by winning."

—Dave Bristol, former Major League baseball manager[1]

The West Region Tournament, played in San Bernardino, California, brought together the state champions from Arizona (Arrowhead Little League), Hawaii (Central East Maui Little League), Nevada (Legacy Little League), Utah (Cedar American Little League), and two representatives from California (Lakeside Little League from Northern California and Park View from Southern California). Among these teams, Hawaii stood out as a formidable opponent, having won two of the last four Little League World Series Championships, including the 2008 edition. Arizona also had a tough team, returning for their second West Regional appearance in a row. Once again, playing the role of underdog but fortified by their previous victories and their growing unity as a team, Park View was slated to play the first game against Utah's representative on August 7, 2009, at Al Houghton Stadium in San Bernardino, California. They also had a home field advantage of sorts, as they had traveled about 2 hours by bus, whereas other teams had long journeys. The team from Post Falls, Idaho, was also in San Bernardino playing in the Northwest Region Tournament. The team from Idaho woke up at 1:30 A.M. to catch a red-eye flight from Spokane, Washington, to Boise, Idaho, then another to Los Angeles/ Ontario International Airport.[2]

The West Region Tournament was the first time the kids were away from their family and friends living in a dorm. The parents were limited to very brief visits, so the coaches became surrogate parents. This would continue through the Little League World Series.

As Cory Graft, Bulla's father, commented, "Oscar and Ric had them in their care for a whole month. The parents were not allowed into the dorms. One coach would have to watch the sick kids while the other coach took the kids to practice. My hat's off to the coaches."[3]

This required implicit trust from the parents, who entrusted their children to the two coaches for one whole month. Fortunately, this was not a problem because of the relationship and bond built between the coaches and the parents from the beginning of the process. But, despite the trust, it was difficult for the parents to be away from their children. Jim Conlin, Nick's father, noted that the separation from the kids was easier for the fathers than the mothers. From Jim's perspective, it was something that needed to happen, something the coaches needed to do. "Their mothers missed them, but this is the opportunity of a lifetime—a rite of passage to help them grow up and become young men."[4]

The coaches also had to make sure the kids did their homework, as the kids had a year-round school schedule. It also helped that Kiko Garcia's mother, Sharon, volunteered to be team mother, helping the coaches handle the awesome task of supervising and caring for 12 growing boys. Although the kids were allowed to call, e-mail, and text their families, the coaches significantly limited this time, so Garcia also became the main source of information for the parents, updating them on the kids' morale and health.[5]

The intensity of media and public attention also increased significantly and would continue to mount as Park View progressed toward the Little League World Series. It was now that Park View began to reap the benefits of their strong team chemistry and bond, cushioning them from pressure and allowing them to let off steam when they needed to. During the Western Region Tournament and the Little League World Series, they spent a lot of time stuck in the dorm, and they had to find creative ways to entertain themselves when they

weren't doing homework. This was a particular challenge, complicated by the coaches' decision to keep the kids indoors because of
the intense heat. Coach Ramirez remembers that the kids were struggling to keep themselves occupied without television, video games, or
any other form of entertainment. Coach Castro and Coach Ramirez
joined the kids in their dorm room and showed them how to get
creative with the materials they had at hand. Between games like
dorm pong, where they tied bedsheets to bunk beds, put a line in
the middle, and hit balls over the sheet, and "the Exorcist," better left
unexplained, the boys were never bored again.[6]

All of this time together could have been divisive, but the players
themselves seemed to revel in the experience. Already close from so
many hours logged on the field together, they only grew closer, cementing a bond that many described as being like family. They truly
enjoyed each other's company and relished the chance to get to know
each other better. This bonding became a crucial factor in their ultimate success.

Luke took the opening pitching assignment for the Green Machine
against the team from Utah. The second batter he faced lined a
home run over the right-field wall to give Utah an early lead. But
as we have seen so many times before, the team from Chula Vista
did not get rattled. The boys from Southern California erupted for
27 runs in the first three innings, and Luke teamed up with Isaiah
on a one-hitter in the four-inning run-rule game. Park View continued to demonstrate its power by belting eight home runs—two
each from Luke, Bulla, and Kiko, and solo homers from Oscar and
Jensen Peterson. Attendance for this Friday's afternoon game was
1,200,[7] a far cry from the 8,550[8] fans who attended their next game
on Sunday against the state champions from Hawaii.

In game two against the Hawaii team from Wailuki, Coach Castro went with Park View's other pitching star—Kiko Garcia. It was
déjà vu all over again as Park View blasted eight more home runs in

another four-inning run-rule game. Kiko and Bulla each belted a pair of home runs, giving them four each in the first two West Region games. Andy, Oscar, Isaiah, and Seth Godfrey also added to the team's record-breaking home run totals. The final score was 15–2. Kiko, Seth, and Andy combined for a two-hitter while striking out eight of the Wailuki batters. In these first two games, the Green Machine had dominated its opponents 42 runs to three and 30 hits to four.

The confidence of the Green Machine continued to grow with every pitch and every swing of the bat, and they began to recover their swagger. For their part, Coaches Ramirez and Castro performed masterfully both on and off the field. But things were starting to get a little more complicated now. The kids were playing in front of much bigger crowds. The press was starting to take notice of this Chula Vista band of brothers that seemed to beat its opponents into submission. And just when they needed it most, the community of San Diego began to rally around the boys.

The coaches also did their part to ensure the players were ready to handle the increased scrutiny. Before each game, they would visit with each of the players and get them to focus on the moment rather than the crowds, the noise, and the television cameras. According to Coach Ramirez, "The first couple of games I would have to scream at the kids to get their heads back in the game, and I didn't give them an inch. We started to build a bubble over us where the noise and everything was blocked out. There were only a couple of times that I had to pull them back into the game."[9]

It helped that the hoopla built gradually, allowing the players to become comfortable with it, including interviews, press conferences, and television during the West Regional Tournament. It also helped that ESPN kept a close eye on the kids and guided them through the entire process. Ramirez remembers, "They did really good about keeping that craziness down. ESPN was in charge of pretty much everything, and they had it all planned out for you and what you had to do, so it wasn't overwhelming at all from that standpoint. We did have a meeting here at 7:00 A.M., another meeting here at 7:30 A.M., batting practice at 10:30 A.M., so we had to keep a schedule to accommodate all of the other teams, but they were really good about the whole thing."[10]

One of the developments that caught Coach Castro unprepared was the miking of one of the coaches. Castro was concerned about having the television mike on him, so he and Coach Ramirez decided that Ramirez would take the spotlight. Coach Castro laughed when he described the situation. "I was not miked up, because I thought I would forget in the heat of the game and say something. They (ESPN) showed a video of what not to do. I said Ric's the teacher; he knows what to say. Watching the video, there were times in some of the games where I was getting ready to talk to the kids, and I waved off Ric when he came over to talk strategy."[11]

With back-to-back wins on Friday and Sunday, the Park View team had to play again Monday evening against Arrowhead Little League from Glendale, Arizona. With game-time temperatures at 85 degrees, Park View once again jumped on its opponent quickly. They scored 13 runs in the first inning over an Arizona team stricken with the flu during the week.

Many of the Arrowhead players were deathly ill the day of the game, and a majority of the team spent the day in the hospital getting treated. Arrowhead was going to forfeit the game against Park View, but they took a team vote and the players wanted to take the field. Isaiah, the third starter for the Park View squad, pitched brilliantly for three and one-third innings before he was removed from the game with a 20–1 lead.

Outside of three uncharacteristic errors, Park View played another flawless game. They also added to the home run total by blasting five more, giving them 21 in three games. Number-two hitter Bulla hit two home runs for the third straight game, while Kiko kept his home run game streak alive with a two-run blast in the fourth inning. Number-six hitter Oscar crushed a right-field grand slam in the first inning and followed with a towering three-run round tripper in the fourth inning to finish the scoring for Park View.

Monday night crowds are usually not well attended, but 5,236[12] came with high expectations to watch balls fly off Park View's bats, an indication of the team's growing popularity. The Green Machine did not disappoint their fans. The team from Arizona, while they did not win the game, showed grit and heart in just being on the field that day.

In the West Region Tournament, the top four teams advance to the semifinal round. After three straight wins, Park View had secured a spot in the final four. They played their fourth game in 5 days in another prime-time game at 8 P.M. against the Legacy Little League team from Las Vegas, Nevada. The Nevada team proved that they were familiar with bright lights as they jumped on Park View starter Seth for five first inning runs. Nevada smashed back-to-back home runs in the inning to give them the early momentum. The crowd of 7,125[13] had come to watch the explosive offense from this Park View team, and they were not disappointed as Andy led off the bottom of the first with a solo home run, his third of four first inning leadoff home runs during the 26 games of the tournament. Two batters later, Luke hit a left field solo home run to the applause of the many Chula Vista fans who drove over 100 miles to support their boys. But after scoring 62 runs in their first three games and only 12 innings of baseball, was the Green Machine stalling at the plate with only two runs in two innings?

The answer was a resounding "no" as they erupted for eight runs over the next three innings on five home runs by four different players. Coach Castro strategically used five pitchers during the first five innings, hoping to keep them all fresh for the single elimination semifinal and championship rounds. The strategy also threw off the Las Vegas squad as they were held scoreless after that first inning five spot. In the bottom of the fifth, the floodgates finally opened as the Park View team did what it does best—score big and score often. They put up six runs on five hits and home runs by Kiko, Bradley, Isaiah, and Seth.

Park View went on to beat Nevada 10–5 and go undefeated in pool play. The Park View team added to its amazing home run total by belting seven more round trippers, giving the team 28 at the West Region, along with 72 runs scored. This awesome display of power created quite a buzz with the media, as such numbers were unheard of at this stage in the tournament, mainly because most teams typically had one or two ace pitchers who precluded such high scoring. Although the Little League Web site concedes that it is impossible to keep records of all of the games leading up to the World Series, it is likely that this is a feat which has never before been accomplished and may never be again.

Of the three other teams to reach the semifinals, Park View had already beaten two of them, Nevada and Arizona. The third team was the Northern California team from the City of Granite Bay that also went undefeated in pool play.

Park View had a rematch with Nevada in the semifinal game. They drew the early game at 4:00 P.M., which meant 90-degree playing conditions. A smaller crowd of 6,300[14] came out to watch the early game. Kiko threw four innings of brilliant baseball, giving up two runs on three hits. Kiko was also the hitting star as he blasted three home runs boosting his West Region total to 10. His teammates contributed with three other home runs, including two from left fielder Isaiah, as Park View routed Nevada 15–2 in four innings. The win set up an all-California final against Granite Bay's Lakeside Little League, the Northern California entry and a team that had allowed only five runs in pool play. Lakeside won a 9–8 sixth inning come-from-behind thriller against Arizona, which had rebounded from its bout with the flu.

The final, televised by ESPN, introduced the rest of the world to the Green Machine and the hometown support for the players kicked into high gear. Fans prepared for the big game by commandeering churches, bars, restaurants, and homes to watch the games in large groups. Just one example was Eastlake Church, which organized a get-together with two big-screen TVs, food and drink, with voluntary donations going to support the Park View families and offset their travel expenses.[15]

Park View came into the championship game undefeated with 34 home runs. Most of the 13,350[16] fans in attendance expected another display of long ball, but this game was a little unusual. Once

A young Nick Conlin

Courtesy of the Conlin Family

Jensen Peterson's T-ball days

Courtesy of the Peterson Family

Markus Melin teeing it up

Courtesy of the Melin Family

Oscar Castro's early baseball days

Courtesy of the Castro Family

A young Seth Godfrey pitching

Courtesy of the Godfrey Family

Young gun Kiko Garcia
Courtesy of Sharon Garcia

Little Luke Ramirez with his first bat
Courtesy of the Ramirez Family

Coach Ramirez college swing

Courtesy of Ric Ramirez

9–10 year old section champs

Courtesy of Andy Rios Sr.

10–11 year old Park View team with flags

Courtesy of Andy Rios Sr.

The Park View "Mohawks"

Courtesy of Sharon Garcia

Park View finally beats nemesis Rancho Santa Margarita

Courtesy of Sharon Garcia

Park View and friends enjoy the moment after beating Rancho Santa Margarita
Courtesy of Sharon Garcia

After winning the So Cal title
Courtesy of Sharon Garcia

Representing the West

Courtesy of James Considine

The Birthplace of Little League Baseball

Courtesy of Sharon Garcia

The Williamsport cafeteria

Courtesy of Sports-Shots by Jim Hazen

Night time at Williamsport

Courtesy of Sports-Shots by Jim Hazen

Andy Rios coming in for the save

Courtesy of Sports-Shots by Jim Hazen

Kiko Garcia enjoying the win

Courtesy of Sharon Garcia

The Bombers hanging with Junior Seau

Courtesy of Sharon Garcia

Taking in the Pacific Life Holiday Bowl parade

Courtesy of Sylvia Porras

Tonight Show with Conan O'Brien

Courtesy of Sharon Garcia

Aiming for the stars

Courtesy of Michelle Mattox

Relaxing before the big shoot

Courtesy of Michelle Mattox

One on One with Jane Mitchell

Courtesy of Michelle Mattox

Dreaming of becoming San Diego Padres

Courtesy of Sharon Garcia

again, Park View scored a lot of runs—11—but they only got six hits. They also collected seven walks, perhaps an indication that the Lakeside pitchers were being more careful with them, and they struck out an uncharacteristic nine times. Perhaps most out of character, the fifth inning that won the game for the Green Machine included only one hit, a two-run double by Oscar Castro.

There were also more home runs hit by Park View. Kiko hit two more to push his already astronomical West Regional total to 12. Andy and Luke added one- and two-run shots respectively. But power was not the deciding factor in this game. The waiting game won out as the team's seven walks demonstrated.

The game was tied 3–3 going into the top of the fifth. Isaiah, who had replaced Luke during Lakeside's three-run third inning, was pitching effectively for Park View. Lakeside's starting pitcher Mitch Hart hit his pitch count after walking Bulla with one out. At this point, Park View decided to wait out Lakeside's relievers, Matt Mc-Cord and Connor Briare, to see if they could throw strikes. McCord threw seven consecutive balls before being relieved by Briare. Briare proceeded to throw the last ball to walk Luke, intentionally walked Kiko to load the bases, and walked Bradley to give Park View a 4–3 lead that they never relinquished. The one hit in the inning, Oscar's double, increased the lead to 6–3. Lakeside made two errors to let in two more runs.

The players felt good that they were able to win this way, instead of overpowering their opponents. "It's good to score like that because in Williamsport, we aren't going to be able to just hit home runs," said Kiko, understanding the importance of taking what a team will give. "We have to be able to take walks, get singles, get doubles, and score like that."[17]

Lakeside hit a solo homer in the bottom of the fifth, but Park View answered with back-to-back dingers by Luke and Kiko in the top of the sixth. Spectacular defensive plays and the strong pitching of Isaiah put the lid on another Park View victory and their fifth flag of the summer. This one was not just another victory. Park View was going to Williamsport. They had made it to the Big Show and a chance to win a sixth—and final—flag—the 2009 Little League World Championship.

"I'm excited, but I'm a little nervous," Isaiah said. "I've never been on a plane before."[18]

"This is big not only for us, but for our community," Coach Castro commented after the game. "Chula Vista has never had a team advance to Williamsport like we have, so everyone is really behind us."[19]

The next time Park View played, they would be in Williamsport going against the Great Lakes champion the following Saturday, but before that, they needed to prepare, and there was no time to spare. Reacting quickly to a situation that was new to him and to the rest of the Park View family, league President Rod Roberto sent an e-mail to the Park View parents just before the championship game, giving them instructions about preparing luggage with "enough clothes until Thursday," when they would arrive in Williamsport. He also advised the parents that the boys would not be allowed to leave the complex after the game, and that there would "be a parent meeting immediately after the game for more details."[20] This was just the beginning of the boys' biggest adventure to date in their young lives.

There was an outpouring of well-wishes and congratulations from friends and opponents. Rod Roberto and the team got some advice from Randy Atkinson, coach of the Oceanside American Little League, the team that had represented the West Region in the 2008 Little League World Series:

> Congratulations on the great run at San Bernardino!!!! Oceanside American wishes your team the best. You will experience something special being there and being around the great people of Williamsport, Pa. Our family went last year, and we got to know the Japan team, and before that at San Bernardino, the Hawaii team. A friend of ours is an "aunt" for one of the teams every year. Keep the players loose and have fun. Downtown there is a place called the "Original Little League"—take your team there one day for an hour or so and throw the ball around and visit the tiny museum.[21]

Torrance Little League's President Steve Gottlieb had this to say:

> On behalf of Torrance Little League and the coaches, players, and parents of our 11–12-year-old All-Star team, I'd like to congratulate your 11–12-year-old All-Star team on winning the West Regional Tournament and advancing to the Little League World Series Tournament! We enjoyed playing your league's team in the three-game Southern California Tournament. It is truly a testament to your teams' "heart" after losing the first game to us 18–0, that they came back to win the next two games to advance to San Bernardino. It is their "never say quit" attitude that propelled them through the West Region, and it was an absolute pleasure to see that. Your players, coaches, and fans were great and showed a lot of class throughout the tournament. The coaches, boys, and families are excellent representatives of your league and your community. We know the experience they will have in Williamsport will last throughout their lifetimes and are very happy for them. We will be rooting for them to make it to the Little League World Series Final. Congratulations again.[22]

After the Park View win, their opponents also had some observations. Pat Schneeman, the Sweetwater coach, said, "They won in a close game against us, and obviously they won other close games. When you win close games, you keep winning close games. When they got into San Bernardino, we thought that they would get smoked. They opened up with Utah, and they destroyed them. And we all said, 'Let's see how they play against Arizona or Hawaii because they are stronger teams.' They mowed through them, and at that point, we said, 'Holy cow, they are going all the way.'"[23]

Brent Rhylick, the Rancho Santa Margarita coach, commented, "When they motored through San Bernardino, that's when we said, 'Okay, maybe they have a chance to go all the way because they never stop hitting that ball.' It was amazing how far they were hitting the ball. Our kids hit the ball far, but it seemed like these balls were going close to 300 feet."[24]

Not everyone was convinced that talent alone was responsible for the record-breaking long ball prowess of the Park View team. As the ugly side of Little League baseball emerged, several individuals accused Park View of doctoring, or "rolling," their bats.

According to Don Norcross of the *San Diego Union-Tribune,* rolling bats is "accomplished by positing the bat between two rollers that apply enough pressure to stretch the bat's fibers, making the bat less dense. As the fibers stretch farther apart, the bat becomes more springy, sometimes described as the trampoline effect." It is strongly discouraged by Little League and other youth baseball organizations because, although it is not technically illegal in itself, it may create a bat that exceeds maximum allowable performance limits, constituting bat doctoring. In essence, it gives players a "hot bat," allowing them to hit the ball farther and harder than a normal bat.[25]

Park View's performance in San Bernardino (36 home runs in six games) got several people speculating about their bats. During the tournament, West Region Tournament Director Jim Gerstenslager said he received an anonymous e-mail, accusing the team of "rolling their bats," although he stated that every team at the West Region Tournament had its bats inspected by umpires before each game and no bats were found to be illegal. "I don't care where the pitch is, these kids get the bat on the ball. That's what makes them outstanding. They hit some monster home runs, for sure," Gerstenslager commented.[26]

Coach Castro and Coach Ramirez also denied the bats had been rolled or doctored in any way. Ramirez said people making accusations against Park View were belittling the hard work put in by the players. He said the players were "putting good swings" on the ball and that they were disciplined, willing to take walks. "Somebody who doesn't know (about the team's work ethic) is going to automatically feel like somebody is cheating," Ramirez said.[27]

Calin Thomas, an executive for Easton, one of the largest bat suppliers, said rolling bats does give them a greater trampoline effect, "but we're not talking about leaps and bounds." He had also heard about people accusing Park View of rolling bats in San Bernardino.[28]

"If this team's hitting a lot of home runs, people want to ignore the fact that they're working hard on their fundamental skills and want to attribute it to something else. It's sad."[29]

Thankfully, the kids were largely unaware of the controversy as they took a new set of bats made by Easton to Williamsport to go about the business of winning a World Championship.

10 | Their Field of Dreams

The 2009 Little League World Series

"Do your best and forget the consequences."
—Walt Alston, Hall of Fame Major League baseball manager[1]

Park View Little League had become the first California District 42 team ever to reach the Little League World Series. But before they boarded a plane to head to Williamsport, there was much preparation, planning, and fundraising to be done.

Although the expenses of the coaches and players were covered by Little League, transporting 12 families cross country is not cheap, and in this case, the estimated cost was about $6,000 per family, or about $80,000 in total. Fortunately, the San Diego community stepped up with generous donations. The Sycuan Tribal Group donated $15,000.[2] XX Sports Radio (1090-AM) raised $22,000 for the team,[3] $10,000 of that amount was contributed by San Diego Padre Owner Jeff Moorad.[4] Several San Diego Padres players stepped up to the plate, pitching in various amounts. Fellow District 42 Little League Chula Vista American generously provided a check for $1,000.[5] Other local radio and TV stations also got into the act. And the community at large donated whatever they could afford. In all, the Chula Vista and San Diego communities raised over $100,000 for the Park View team.

The Park View board facilitated much of this fundraising activity. Many of them stayed behind when the team went to Williamsport, seeking donations, helping make travel reservations, setting up game-watching events, printing flyers, and even buying new equipment for the team. They were amazed and gratified by the tremendous out-pouring of support from the community. In fact, it was so tremendous that between the time the team won the Western Region Tournament on August 16, and the time they stepped on the plane on August 17, they had all the funds they needed.

The players and their families boarded three separate planes on the morning of Monday, August 17. It was Isaiah Armenta's and Markus Melin's first flight ever. The media appeared en masse at Los Angeles/Ontario International Airport, where they began their long journey. Their itinerary took them to Houston, Texas, and Newark, New Jersey, before arriving in South Williamsport. Along the way, fellow passengers asked the players for autographs. They were joined by the Northwest Region Championship team from Mercer Island, Washington, and one of the flight attendants introduced both teams over the PA system. As an added bonus, for $6, some of the players got to watch the replay of their 11–4 victory over Northern California to win the Western Regional Championship. It was the first time any of them had seen it.[6]

After arriving in Newark, the team boarded a bus that took them to Williamsport, Pennsylvania. It was a long drive, some 179 miles mostly west on Interstate 80 across the Pennsylvania countryside, all but invisible to the players because of the darkness. Near the end of the journey, the bus exited I-80 for a northward jog on US-15, about 17 miles. Finally, after the long journey, they arrived in Williamsport around 1:30 A.M. on Tuesday, August 18, almost a full day after they had departed their hometown. It was worth the wait as they beheld Howard J. Lamade Stadium, lit up in all its glory. "It was like a Field of Dreams," according to little Oscar Castro.[7] The buses dropped the

kids at the dorms that would be their homes for what they hoped
would be all 13 days of the Series.

The Williamsport complex was more spacious and accommodating than the team had experienced in San Bernardino. The coaches
each had a dorm room and their own showers and were separated
from the players by a hallway. The players each had a bunk. Four teams
stayed in each of the four dorm buildings, with one international
and one United States team on each floor. Park View drew Canada
on its floor and the United Arab Emirates along with the U.S. East
Coast team stayed on the second floor. The dorms formed a circle
around the rest of the facilities, including a pool, a game room, and a
cafeteria.[8]

The ever-diligent team mother, Sharon Garcia, had arrived in
advance of the rest of the parents and took advantage of a visit to drop
off supplies to Coaches Castro and Ramirez. She also did some scout-
ing of the facilities and evaluated the accommodations so she could
report back to the players' families. She found that the Williamsport
compound "was much more secure than San Bernardino." She was
thrilled to know that Williamsport designates two "uncles" to each
team. An uncle is a local person from the town of Williamsport who
guides them through the activities for the week.[9] In an e-mail to the
Park View parents, Sharon's descriptions provided a detailed account
of the thrills—and challenges—the boys and the coaches faced:

> I totally lucked into seeing the boys yesterday. I was dropping
> off the supplies that Ric and Oscar had asked me to pick up at
> the store, and Ric had to meet me at the guard gate. He told me
> they were getting ready to take their official ESPN pictures so if
> I wanted to wait, they would be outside in a bit. We waited out-
> side the guard gate, and the boys took the pictures on the grass
> near the stadium where we were waiting. The photographer said
> we couldn't take pictures, but one of the uncles told Alexa she
> could quickly take one with her phone so that is the one I sent
> out. She would like to get a photo credit (ha-ha). There are three
> uncles assigned to our team who assist Oscar and Ric and help

out with the boys. They are really nice guys who have worked the Little League World Series for years.

The dorms appear to be much nicer and Ric and Oscar both commented that they have their own living quarters adjacent to the boys with their own bathrooms so they are happy! There is a TV room, game room with video games, swimming pool, etc., so there is a lot more to do here. All of the practice fields and batting cages are on-site. The boys all seemed very happy and excited. They were all troopers throughout the long day of travel, and although Jensen and Markus were not feeling 100 percent while traveling, yesterday both looked great. Ric and Oscar found out they have to wear dress slacks to all of the games, so they had to make a quick run to the store with another team to get outfitted. Pretty funny seeing them all dressed up in their spiffy duds!

The boys are busy enjoying themselves and are kept busy, so we may not hear from them much, but from what I could see, they are SO happy and living the dream!

Weather is overcast and muggy. I'm going to the store today because the boys would like some bug spray, so you may want to bring some for yourselves.

Have a safe trip, and I will see all of you in Williamsport!

Still can't believe our boys will be playing in the LITTLE LEAGUE WORLD SERIES![10]

The teams visited the game room extensively. That was one of the differences between San Bernardino and Williamsport. Another difference was that Coach Castro and Coach Ramirez let the kids leave the dorm rooms more to play and blow off steam, primarily because of the temperature difference. In San Bernardino, it was blazing hot, whereas the Williamsport weather was cool. Oscar Castro remembers how much the players loved the game room. What sticks in his mind particularly is the video game *Wii Little League*. In his words, "We were all over that game."[11]

One of Luke's biggest memories of Williamsport was the cafeteria where they ate most of their meals. With a bit of awe in his voice, he shares, "Being in the cafeteria, there's a wall where they have the pictures of the all of the teams that have won the Little League World Series. Every time we ate there, I always looked at all of the teams before we left. It was hard to believe that we could end up on that wall too." He used the wall as a motivator to sustain his push toward his ultimate goal—winning the championship.[12]

They could not see it the night they arrived, but the players and their families had arrived in a beautiful little valley, one of many in the lovely state of Pennsylvania. It was dotted with pines and other trees. In fact, until the late 1890s, Williamsport sustained itself through sawmills and furniture factories, which devastated tree growth in the area. Nowadays, the forests have come back and there is no dominant industry. Little League Baseball, Inc., contributes significantly to the Williamsport community, with 100 employees and approximately $30 million in annual revenue, but it is only one component of a thriving economy. Other significant employers include the Pennsylvania College of Technology, a branch campus of Pennsylvania State University; Lycoming College, founded in 1812, and one of the oldest liberal arts colleges in the U.S.; Shop-Vac, which has its international headquarters in Williamsport; Textron, a Boeing company; and Susquehanna Health System.[13] The city counts around 40,000 residents.[14]

In many ways, Williamsport is a typical small town. When you get a haircut, everyone knows it. On the other hand, the annual spectacle of the Little League World Series has turned it into a "big" little town. When the Series is taking place, people come from all over to see the parade and the games, and the crowds are huge. It was that way on Thursday, August 20, when the players attended the Grand Slam Parade, which wound its way through downtown Williamsport and introduced the 16 tournament entrants to the folks of Williamsport and South Williamsport. Opening ceremonies were held on Friday, August 21, which was also the first day of games but an off-day for Park View. In his daily blog, league President Roberto commented, "Overall, the kids seem in good spirits. The moms think that the kids miss them, but in reality, the kids are having the time of their lives."[15]

Before their first game, one of Coach Ramirez's objectives was to work with his son Luke on his pitching. Ramirez got a call from a friend after the final that Luke pitched in San Bernardino. Luke didn't have a very good outing and had difficulty locating his pitches. Coach Ramirez hadn't watched his son throw in the pen for a while and his friend offered some advice. "It looks like Luke is coming down and crossing his body a little bit as he is throwing." Coach Ramirez recalls, "I worked the bullpen and opened Luke up and boom, boom, boom. He pitched well after that."[16]

After interviews, uniform fittings, and other pregame preparations, Park View was ready to get down to business. This was their toughest challenge in a steady stream of challenges. The 2009 Little League World Series entrants boasted some awesome teams. The Texas team from McAllister had yet to lose a game in 3 years of All-Star tournament play and represented a traditionally strong state with two Little League World Series Championships and five runner-ups in its long history. The Georgia team from Warner Robins was also undefeated 3 years running, had won the championship in 2007, and was vying to collect the fourth championship for its home state. People from Warner Robins liked to refer to their town as "Baseball USA." And then there was Chinese Taipei, the team with 17 world championships to its credit, over 20 percent of the total championships ever awarded. California teams were 0–7 against Chinese Taipei in finals going back to Santa Clara's 5–0 loss in 1969, losing by a combined score of 69–6. Only one of those teams had scored more than one run against Chinese Taipei. Compare that to San Diego teams, that only had one championship to their name, and Chula Vista teams, that had none. In this tournament, the Blue Bombers were truly the underdog.

Their opening game was the final game of the second day of the Little League World Series. This Saturday night 8:00 P.M. affair was against Logan County/Russellville Little League from Kentucky at the main venue—Lamade Stadium. Televised on ESPN2 for the entire world to watch, this game drew 19,500[17] fans. By comparison, Pennsylvania's own Pirates drew only 1,709 more fans the next day at PNC Park in Pittsburgh.[18] The boys had reached the big time.

Millions of fans would be watching to see some of the raw power they had exhibited up to this point. How would they fare with all of the media hype and pressure of the big stage?

The boys from Chula Vista debuted their blue West uniforms (effectively transforming themselves from the Green Machine to the Blue Bombers) in typical fashion by scoring two first inning runs off Bradley's triple. Two innings later, Luke hit a towering leadoff solo home run over the 225-foot right-field fence. This was the tip of the iceberg as the Blue Bombers totaled six home runs and batted around twice while scoring 12 runs in the fourth and fifth innings. The seven round trippers were the most in one game since the Little League World Series expanded to 16 teams in 2001. The previous mark was set in 2005, when Asia Region Champion Musashi-Fuchu hit five.[19] Included in the inning were back-to-back-to-back home runs by Isaiah, Seth, and Andy who were hitting eighth, ninth, and first in the batting order. Overshadowed by the powerful hitting display was the one-hit baseball thrown by ace Kiko Garcia. The lone hit was a slow grounder off the bat of cleanup hitter Ian Woodall between the mound and third base. The final score of this opening game was 15–0. The Blue Bombers pounded out 17 hits, including 12 from the first five hitters in their lineup.

The Blue Bombers played their second game at Volunteer Stadium against the New England representative Peabody Western Little League. Volunteer Stadium was opened in 2001 to accommodate the growth of the Little League World Series.[20] Its approximate capacity is 10,000, a far cry from the 40,000 at Lamade Stadium. The fans in Volunteer Stadium are almost exclusively in the main stands, with limited lawn seating in the outfield. Volunteer Stadium is used for early-round and tournament consolation games.

Just over 10,000[21] fans crammed Volunteer Stadium to help count the home runs off the Blue Bomber bats. But it wasn't home runs being counted at this game—instead, it was the "*K*." This was a pitcher's duel as the six hurlers combined for 24 strikeouts. The Blue Bombers didn't have much of an answer for Peabody's pitcher Matt Hosman.

"That one was uncomfortable," said Coach Castro after the game. "He pretty much just challenged us. You gotta tip your cap to him."[22]

Seth's single up the middle scored pinch runner Nick Conlin for what would be the game-winning run. The Bombers were held to only three hits in the first four innings. They also struck out an unusual eight times in those innings. The boys of Chula Vista finally got back to the long ball they were so used to in the fifth inning, as third baseman Seth took a 1–1 offering over the heads of outfield spectators in left-center to give Park View a 2–0 lead.

In the top of the sixth, the Blue Bomber bats finally came alive with a vengeance. Oscar hit a leadoff double and crossed home plate two pitches later on an RBI single into right center field off the bat of Junior Porras. Peabody's Matt Correale answered by retiring the next two batters in order. But as they did so many times before, the Blue Bomber bats would score 11 more runs during this 17 batter inning, including two dingers by Andy. The final score was 14–0, the win assuring Park View a spot in the United States semifinals alongside their next opponent, McAllister Park American Little League from San Antonio, Texas.

Coaches Castro and Ramirez were satisfied with this style of victory. It was yet another way the Blue Bombers could win a game.

The final game of pool play at Williamsport would determine who earned the number-one seed in Pool B. Two undefeated teams, Park View and the Southwest representative from Texas, squared off at Howard J. Lamade Stadium in front of 22,750[23] fans and another ESPN2 television audience.

Not letting the baseball world down, the Blue Bombers scored two runs in the bottom of the first inning as Kiko slugged his second home run of the World Series. It was a towering two-run blast that landed just past and to the right of the "*W*" on the "LITTLE LEAGUE WORLD SERIES" banner on the center-field hill.

Asked if he was nervous after the Garcia home run—Chula Vista had hit 10 home runs in its first two games—San Antonio manager Mike Shull shook his head.

"Not at all," he said. "Since we were already advancing, we were going to have a little bit of fun."[24]

The team from Texas gave its own power display with a two-run triple by Drew Brooks and a massive solo home run by the next batter Travis Daves that traveled the same distance as Garcia's earlier blast. Southwest tacked on two more runs off the home run by Wyatt Willis, their 5-foot-3, 95-pound center fielder. When it was over, the Blue Bombers had lost for the first time in 24 days. The boys in blue's three runs and seven hits were their fewest in the Williamsport tourney so far. In their previous two games, they had outscored opponents 29–0 and outhit them 32–7. The good news—the Blue Bombers were assured at least one more game, and Coach Castro had plenty of pitching available for the single elimination semifinal game against the number-one seed from Pool A—Warner Robins from Georgia.

According to Coach Castro, "The players were getting ahead of themselves, talking about the home run record, and their swings started to change toward home runs. If we had won the Texas game, I feel we would have lost the championship. After that loss, they were ready to listen again and go back to the game plan."[25]

Kasey Ramirez, Luke's mother, also felt that this loss was one of the key moments of the Series for the Blue Bombers. At this point, she felt Park View was rolling over teams with ease and they were getting too comfortable and somewhat overconfident.[26]

"Without that loss happening, it could have been a much more difficult Series. It was a blessing in disguise."[27]

Heading into the U.S. semifinal elimination game, the Park View team used their off day to get back to fundamentals. After the Texas loss, Coach Castro and Coach Ramirez had the players' attention and got them to go back to the basics. In their past successes, they were not trying to hit home runs. The goal was always double digits in the hit column. If they did that, they felt they were going to win.[28] Once again, Coaches Castro and Ramirez made them hit Wiffle balls, a strategy that helped them after their last loss against Torrance.[29]

Park View's semifinal opponent was the powerhouse from Georgia—Warner Robins Little League. Warner Robins has a notable history in Little League baseball. Claude Lewis, the director of the Warner Robins Recreation Department, is widely regarded as the inventor of the game of T-ball.[30] On August 26, 2007, the U.S. champion from Warner Robins defeated the international champion from Tokyo, Japan, 3–2, in eight innings on a walk-off home run to win the 2007 Little League World Series.[31]

Two years and 1 day later, Warner Robins attempted to reach their second U.S. finals game in 3 years. Park View sent ace pitcher Kiko Garcia to the mound, and he looked unbeatable after three innings, giving up only one run on two base hits. Before the game, Coaches Castro and Ramirez made a change in the batting lineup by switching Bulla and Kiko. "The main thing we were trying to do is protect Garcia," Coach Castro said about the lineup change. "With Luke right behind him, we just felt that he was going to get more pitches."[32] The coaching strategy paid off as the hot-hitting Kiko went four for four in the game. The Blue Bombers provided the offensive support in the bottom of the third by blasting two home runs and taking a 5–1 lead. In the fourth, Warner Robins got to Kiko early. Isaiah relieved Kiko after four batters, but it wasn't Isaiah's day as he gave up six runs in only one-third of an inning. Reliable Andy Rios came in to close out the nine-run fourth inning for Warner Robins.

"We were thinking we weren't really done," Andy recollected of Chula Vista's mindset in the dugout after the nine-run inning. "We play all six innings 100 percent. We were kind of down, but we got our momentum up and scored."[33]

Down 10–5, the Blue Bombers started to chip away and scored two runs in the fourth inning on a two-run homer by Kiko. Oscar opened the fifth inning with a triple and scored on Junior's single to center field. When Andy blasted a dramatic three-run homer over the center-field fence, the 21,000[34] in attendance and the millions of ESPN2 viewers at home were left with a 10–10 tie through five innings. Andy followed up with his second scoreless inning to set up a dramatic bottom of the sixth. After 20 runs and 25 hits between the two teams, Park View notched the winning run when pinch runner Nick Conlin scored from third on a Conner Smith wild pitch. With the come-from-behind win, Park View had a rematch with the team from Texas that defeated them 6–3 in the Pool B finale. After the game, Warner Robins Coach Randy Jones had high praise for the Blue Bombers.

"You're never comfortable against those guys," said Jones, whose team had yet to lose in All-Star play before this U.S. semifinal. "They're just explosive. You can't pitch around everybody. What a great team, maybe the best I've ever seen."[35]

One game would determine if the Chula Vista Blue Bombers could become just the fourth team from San Diego to reach the coveted Little League World Series final and the second team to win it all. The 1957 and 1977 teams from El Cajon, California, were runner-ups, while the 1961 La Mesa team was the only champion to date.

Rainy weather, unusual for this time of the year, moved the start time for the game from 3:00 P.M. to 7:00 P.M. Besides the fact that Park View had a chance to win the United States championship, the night was special for another reason. League President Rod Roberto had promised to fly Sal Vega to this game if Park View defeated Warner Robins. Vega, who was now in his 80s, had been volunteering at Park View Little League since the beginning, 1969. Roberto made good on his promise, and Vega had a seat to watch the biggest game in Park View's history to date.[36]

When the game finally got underway, the West Region Champions banged out nine runs in the bottom of the first inning in their

rematch with Texas. They hit three home runs in the inning, a towering two-run blast by starting pitcher Luke, a solo shot by Bulla, and
a grand slam by lead-off hitter, Andy. The inning ended eventually,
but not before 14 players had batted and everybody in the starting
lineup had either reached base or recorded an RBI. In the third inning, Bulla's second home run of the game pushed Park View's run
total to 12. Bulla's blast further justified his manager's choice to slot
him in the fourth spot.

Luke was masterful on the mound as he pitched a four-inning,
six-strikeout, one-hit, and one-earned-run game. Texas fought for
two runs in the top of the fourth, but the 12–2 lead earned the Blue
Bombers a mercy rule win that proclaimed them United States champions and gave them the opportunity to represent their country in the
final.

"I mean, I never thought I'd hear those words about our team
when we first started this thing," Chula Vista Manager Oscar Castro
said. "But it sounds good. I like it."[37]

"This is an awesome feeling right now," pitcher Ramirez said.
"This team has been together since we were 7 or 8 years old, and
we've all known each other. We're practically family; we're all brothers
out there, and we get to share this together."[38]

Through their five games, the Blue Bombers hit a Little League
World Series record 19 homers, breaking the previous mark of 15 set
in 2003 by Musashi-Fuchu Little League from Tokyo, Japan. Would
they add to that record in the final?

Park View's championship appearance marked the twenty-first time
a team from California had made the finals. However, it was only
the fourth time a team from baseball-rich San Diego County had
made it this far. San Diego County debuted in Williamsport in 1957,
when La Mesa Northern Little League was shut out by Angel Macias
and the team from the Monterrey Industrial Little League, Monterrey, Mexico, 4–0 in the only perfect game ever pitched in the Little

League Baseball World Series Championship game. The team from Monterrey also became the first team from outside the U.S. to win the Little League Baseball World Series. Ironically, a motion picture called *The Perfect Game* was released in April of 2010, which tells the story of this historic team. In fact, the Blue Bombers were treated to an advance screening of the movie, cheering throughout. San Diego's only previous championship came in 1961 when a team from Northern El Cajon prevailed over El Campo, Texas, 4–2. The region would not be represented in the title game again until 1977, when it lost to the representative from Chinese Taipei 7–2.[39] The 2009 game set up a San Diego County–Chinese Taipei rematch 32 years in the making.

The largest crowd of the tournament arrived at Howard J. Lamade Stadium to watch the record-breaking Blue Bombers from Chula Vista face the boys from Asia-Pacific Taoyuan, Chinese Taipei. Approximately 32,400[40] fans crammed the hillside to see if the Blue Bombers could become the first California team to take the Little League Baseball World Series title since the team from Long Beach won in 1993. The game would be played in front of the ABC television crew, which included legendary lead broadcaster Brent Musberger. The coaches purposely kept the routine the same before the big game. The only difference in their message was to let the boys know that they were playing for the championship and that they should go for it because they had nothing to lose.[41]

Reliable Isaiah received the starting nod on the mound for the United States champions from Chula Vista. Isaiah sailed through the first few innings, but Chinese Taipei jumped on him the second time around when Wen Hua Sung lined a two-out, two-run home run to give the Asia-Pacific champs an early 2–0 advantage. The next batter, cleanup hitter Chin Ou, hit a solo home run to right field. After the second home run, Kiko took the mound and struck out the next batter to end the inning. The Blue Bombers scored a run of their own in the third on Kiko's double to center field. Kiko shut down Chinese Taipei 1–2–3 in the top of the fourth, a huge momentum swing for the U.S. team. Now the Blue Bombers needed to get the offense in gear.

Jensen Peterson and Nick Conlin, who had entered the game as defensive replacements in the top of the fourth, made their biggest contributions to the cause. Jensen led off with a single, and Nick followed with a double to right field, which put runners on second and third. Seth, the team's number-nine hitter, lofted a sacrifice fly to center field to bring his team to within a run. Nick scored on a wild pitch to knot it up at 3–3. Bulla later singled to right scoring Andy and giving Park View a 4–3 lead at the end of the fourth.

With almost four million fans watching this championship game around the world, and 32,400 fans in the stadium shouting "USA ... USA," the adrenaline was flowing. Kiko was so pumped up that he became unusually erratic. The Blue Bombers' ace pitcher hit a pair of batters and walked another to fill the bags with one out. Chinese Taipei's cleanup man Chin Ou came to the plate to face Kiko for the first time. His last at bat was a solo home run in the third. With the count 1–2, the Blue Bomber defense provided some fireworks of its own. Ou ripped the ball between third base and shortstop. Third baseman Seth was guarding the line defensively, and it appeared Ou's hit would end up in left field to score the tying run. But shortstop Andy grabbed the ball, tagged the runner going to third, and fired to first for an inning-ending double play. The momentum quickly shifted to Park View. The fans erupted once again with their "USA" cheer as the Blue Bombers sprinted to their dugout for their next at bat.

"What was going through my mind was that coach wanted corners in, and most of the batters that Kiko faced were up on him," Andy said. "So I was cheating toward third base, and that's where he hit it. I just tagged the runner and threw to first. The momentum was on their side when they had the bases loaded. But after I turned that double play, it was all ours."[42]

The Blue Bombers tacked on two more runs on four hits in the bottom of the fifth for a 6–3 lead. It was the first game in this tournament that the Blue Bombers had failed to homer and only the second game overall. But championship teams find ways to win, and Park View did just that. Needing just three more outs, Kiko struck out the side, completing three and one-third innings of no-hit relief baseball. After he threw the final pitch and saw the outcome, Kiko fell to his knees. Luke and fellow teammates sprinted to the mound. Gloves and hats flew. Fists pumped. With this 6–3 victory, the team from Park View Little League in Chula Vista, California, had made yet another comeback, and had overcome more obstacles to complete an amazing journey witnessed by millions throughout the world. They secured their sixth and final flag and were proclaimed World Champions. With this championship, they realized a dream many of them had since the age of 3 or 4 when they joined their first T-ball team. They accomplished something that only a handful of the millions of kids who play Little League baseball ever experience.

"It's just amazing to be called World Champions," said Andy, who went 3-for-3 with an RBI in the game. "We just wanted to come in here and just try to go for it, and we did. It's just an amazing feeling."[43]

"We knew we would come back because we knew we could hit any type of pitching," Kiko said. "We knew we could come back. We always do."[44]

"I think they've matured a lot as we've gone on," Coach Castro said. "But I think there have been some key losses as we've gone on that have helped these boys mature a little bit quicker so they wouldn't get so hot and think they were invincible. These guys have a lot of character, and coming back from that, even as a coach, you really feel that they can. But there's always that little voice that you just kind of think, 'To come back from that type of a loss, can they *really* do it?' They proved me wrong every time."[45]

A little later, after Coach Castro had a little time to reflect, he added this. "No matter what happens, no matter what you accomplish, you can always say that you won the Series. Not many people can say that."[46]

Epilogue

"Baseball was, is, and always will be, to me, the best game in the world."

—Babe Ruth[1]

Victory was sweet, but the Blue Bombers had little time to savor it before plunging headfirst into a series of public appearances and love fests with their fans.

It started immediately, with e-mails and letters pouring in such as this e-mail from a 60-year-old grandfather from Spring Valley in San Diego, which does a great job of summing up why the Blue Bombers captivated so many people:

> Why are so many people that you don't know so excited for you? Yes, we appreciate that you made history as true "World" Champions, something even Major League baseball, pro football, or basketball can't claim. You won something equivalent to the Olympics on the world stage.
>
> But aside from that, think of these things. I'm a typical 60-year-old grandpa who played baseball in the streets, fields, and parks as soon as I could hold a ball. The Little League fields I played on in Lemon Grove are still there. I played on All-Stars just like you, coached All-Star teams like yours, and experienced the thrill of advancing from area to district, and so on, like you did. The difference is you continued to win and we didn't.
>
> One reason so many people are so happy for you is that we were able to be with you in the batter's box or on the field and share the experience with you. Many people remember being part of a team sport where so many things have to go right to make it to the top. As for me,

I was able to be part of your hit that scored a run or make the right coaching decision that may have won the game.

I hope you all take time to thank God for allowing you to be part of this incredible experience and that baseball fans everywhere could share it with you. Thanks for the memories.[2]

Right after their victory, California Governor Arnold Schwarzenegger published a statement congratulating the team.

"Chula Vista broke records, showed remarkable sportsmanship, and persevered throughout the Series, and I am proud to say they are from California."[3]

Chula Vista Mayor Cheryl Cox threw in her two cents.

"Our boys of summer are world champions, and we're going to throw a world-class celebration for them. The Blue Bombers have lifted the spirits of the city and the entire region, and we can't wait to cheer for them."[4]

The event she referred to was a gathering at Southwestern College's DeVore Stadium to welcome the boys back from Williamsport and celebrate their tremendous accomplishment. On that night, a Monday, approximately 8,000 fans and well-wishers packed the stadium, some of the crowd waiting more than 2 hours for the team to return from their trip.[5]

When they arrived at a little before 10 P.M., the crowd went nuts, taking it to a new decibel level when comedian George Lopez appeared unexpectedly and led the stadium in chanting—"We are— Park View."[6]

Something was scheduled for every day of that first week back. On Tuesday, the boys were special guests of the San Diego Chargers for a practice session. They watched the Chargers scrimmage, and they mingled with their heroes. For their part, the Chargers were as impressed by the Blue Bombers as everyone else.

"It was awesome," Charger great LaDainian Tomlinson said. "Watching those guys do what they did, being the best in the world, man, it was pretty sweet that they were right here in San Diego. Having the chance to meet them was even better."[7]

Although the players were dwarfed by the giant football players, Luke is so tall that he nearly measured up.[8]

"I was so excited that we got to come out and see all these guys," said Luke, who is too big to play Pop Warner football. "I knew they were going to be loose and stuff, and practice was going to be really fun. I definitely enjoy watching these guys every Sunday. They're my favorite team."[9]

The Chargers went on to honor Park View at their home opener against the Baltimore Ravens on September 20, 2009.[10]

On Wednesday, the players returned to school and were showered with an assembly in their honor. That night, the Bombers had dinner with Adrian Gonzales, the San Diego Padre All-Star. On Thursday night, the team hit the big time with an appearance on *The Tonight Show with Conan O'Brien*. On Friday, they attended another rally of more than 10,000 people. So many fans wanted to attend that they had to move the event from the City's Memorial Park to the Southwestern College football stadium.

The rally started with the arrival of the kids on Ladder Truck 57 from the Chula Vista Fire Department. Numerous local, state, and federal elected officials, representatives of sponsors, and former San Diego Padres Phil Nevin and Randy Jones awaited the kids on stage.[11]

The first week was a whirlwind. And that was just the beginning. Wherever the Blue Bombers went, people recognized them, adored them, and wanted their autographs. The boys treated everyone as they had been taught—with respect. Each of them had slightly different reactions to the adulation they received.

Oscar:	"I try to feel like the same person, but at the same time, I wanted to enjoy it because it only happens once."[12]
Luke:	"When I get bigheaded, my mom keeps me in check."[13] (By the way, Luke's mom says that was never a worry.)
Bradley:	"I try to enjoy the moment and all of the attention."[14]
Junior:	"We felt like rock stars. It was really hard to keep it in perspective."[15]

Seth:	"After we won, we felt like celebrities; we were treated like royalty. It was crazy."[16]
Isaiah:	"The coaches taught us not to let it go to our head—to stay humble."[17]
Markus:	"The attention felt really good, meeting new people and celebrities. It was a once-in-a-lifetime opportunity."[18]
Jensen:	"We make sure we don't act cocky, and we remember to respect people when we appear in public."[19]

Despite the challenges the boys alluded to, one of the hallmarks of this group of players is that they have not let this attention and adulation go to their heads. They continue to practice what their parents have taught them—humbleness and respect. And the honors continue. They appeared in the Mother Goose Parade, an annual tradition in El Cajon, California. They have met athletes and celebrities like Kobe Bryant and George Lopez. They anchored a float in the grand old Rose Bowl Parade on New Year's Day. Many companies have stepped up to sponsor them. And they received an invitation to visit the White House, meeting with President Obama on Friday, February 5, 2010. The president greeted each boy and shook his hand, a dream come true that most people will never realize.

On March 13, 2010, the boys came full circle as Park View Little League held its 2010 opening-day ceremony. On a stage erected at home plate, the team greeted this year's entries and their families and friends, and received their Championship Rings. They earned congratulations from Bob Chandler, legendary San Diego Padres broadcaster; David Wells, former New York Yankee; and San Diego Padre and native San Diegan Billy Ray Smith, radio personality, and former San Diego Charger linebacker; and Jane Mitchell, Channel 4 San Diego reporter and namesake of *One on One with Jane Mitchell*, a 22-time Emmy Award-winning show that has hosted greats such as Ted Williams and Tony Gwynn. Mitchell later aired a one-hour show dedicated to the Cinderella story of the Blue Bombers and has included them in her book recapping her career and capturing many of the interviews she has conducted over her career.

The ceremony was poignant, joyous, and fitting, never more so than when the Blue Bombers high-fived the young T-ball players who dream of one day winning the Little League World Series and look to the Blue Bombers as heroes. It was a day of beginnings and ends—the beginning of a Little League baseball career for the T-ball players and the end for the 12 Blue Bombers as they prepare to go off to new schools and new teams—but they will always have Williamsport 2009 to keep them together, if only in spirit.

Beyond awards and recognition, the Blue Bombers' victory may have more lasting consequences. With the world opening up to them, they may be able to receive an education from some of the area's private high schools, some of which have first-class baseball programs. If so, it would be a fitting result for a group of kids who highly value education.

What are some of the messages the team and its families want to take from this whole experience?

Luke says, "I want us to be remembered for how much heart we had. Through all those games, losing to Torrance in the Southern California Division Championship and battling back to win back-to-back games in Encino, it would just be a great honor to be remembered as the team that brought the championship back to San Diego."[20]

It is refreshing to hear Luke describe their experience using the word "honor." It is remarkable to see an attitude like that in today's world, especially from a 13-year-old.

His mother Kasey raves about the community support, noting how incredible it was. "The best part was when we got back and saw true joy in people's faces—especially because it is hard times for everyone."[21]

Isaiah is matter-of-fact about how he wants the team to go down in history, wanting people to see that the team was humble and did its talking on the field. Most of all, he wants people to know that they gave "100 percent on every pitch."[22]

Jim Conlin believes the Blue Bombers were not about any one player and that each kid had a vital role and contributed to the victory. "They couldn't have done it without every single player."[23]

Perhaps Marcus puts it most succinctly. "This was a once-in-a-lifetime opportunity."[24]

In the end, we return to the San Diego Hall of Champions where we found the team at the beginning of this story. Since we first met them, the players have been honored extensively and have started to get on with their lives. Will members of this team end up on the Breitbard Hall of Fame wall? It does not really matter one way or the other, because they have already brought a once-in-a-lifetime honor to a hometown that has honored them and shown gratitude to its native sons. And the team has graciously accepted that gift with respect and dignity. That is all Coaches Castro and Ramirez ever asked. And the Blue Bombers delivered.

Appendix

Recap of Tournaments[1]

California District 42 Tournament–Double Elimination (July 5 through July 12)

Hosts—Luckie Waller Little League (San Diego) and Park View Little League (Chula Vista)
Championship game—Park View Little League (Chula Vista)

Game 1–Chula Vista National 4, Southwest 3

Game 2–Chula Vista American 11, South Bay 0

Game 3–Sweetwater Valley 8, Eastlake 0

Game 4–Park View 16, Luckie Waller 0 (HRs–Garcia)

Game 5–Imperial Beach 16, Chula Vista National 7

Game 6–South Bay 12, Southwest 11 (eliminated)

Game 7–Sweetwater Valley 12, Chula Vista American 0

Game 8–Park View 17, Imperial Beach 1 (HRs–Garcia (2), Graft, Ramirez (2), Godfrey)

Game 9–Luckie Waller 13, Chula Vista National 3 (eliminated)

Game 10–Eastlake 16, South Bay 1 (eliminated)

Game 11–Luckie Waller 11, Chula Vista American 1 (eliminated)

Game 12–Eastlake 8, Imperial Beach 7 (eliminated)

Game 13–Park View 8, Sweetwater Valley 1 (HRs–Rios, Ramirez (2), Peterson)

Game 14–Luckie Waller 9, Eastlake 8 (eliminated)

Game 15–Sweetwater Valley 4, Luckie Waller 3 (eliminated)

Game 16–Sweetwater Valley 10, Park View 7 (HRs–Graft, Rios)

TITLE Game–Park View 8, Sweetwater Valley 2 (eliminated) (HRs–Rios, Castro, Peterson)

California Section 7 Tournament–Double Elimination (July 18 through July 21)

Host—Lemon Grove Little League (District 66)

Game 1–Rancho San Diego 17, Lemon Grove 1

Game 2–Park View 8, Brawley 5 (HRs–Graft, Ramirez, Garcia (2), Godfrey)

Game 3–Lemon Grove 7, Brawley 6 (eliminated)

Game 4–Park View 9, Rancho San Diego 1 (HRs–Graft, Garcia, Porras)

Game 5–Lemon Grove 9, Rancho San Diego 8 (eliminated)

TITLE Game–Park View 5, Lemon Grove 3 (Eliminated) (HRs–Rios, Porras, Armenta)

Southern California–South Subdivisional–Double Elimination (July 24 through 29)

Host—Clairemont Little League (San Diego) (District 32)
At Cadman Community Park

Game 1–Rancho Santa Margarita 20, Upland Foothill 3

Game 2–Park View 14, Corona National 4 (HRs–Rios (2), Graft)

Game 3–Rancho Santa Margarita 10, Mission Trails 0 (4 innings)

Game 4–Corona National 18, Upland Foothill 7 (6 innings; eliminated)

Game 5–Park View 5, Rancho Santa Margarita 4 (7 innings) (HRs–Ramirez)

Game 6–Mission Trails 7, Corona National 2 (eliminated)

Game 7–Rancho Santa Margarita 7, Mission Trails 4 (eliminated)

TITLE Game–Park View 16, Rancho Santa Margarita 1 (Eliminated) (HRs–Rios, Graft (2), Ramirez, Garcia, Roberto, Godfrey (2))

Southern California Championship Series–Double Elimination (August 1 through August 3)

Host—Encino Little League (District 40)

Game 1–Torrance 18, Park View 0 (4 innings) (HRs–none)

Game 2–Park View 7, Torrance 6 (HRs–Ramirez, Garcia)

TITLE Game–Park View 19, Torrance 12 (Eliminated) (HRs–Rios, Ramirez, Roberto (2), Godfrey (2))

West Region Tournament–Pool Play (August 7 through August 16)

Host—Little League Western Region Headquarters, San Bernardino, California
At Al Houghton Stadium

Game 1–Park View (Southern California) 27, Cedar American (Utah) 1 (4 innings) (HRs–Ramirez (2), Castro, Garcia (2), Peterson, Graft (2))

Game 2–Arrowhead (Arizona) 7, Central East Maui (Hawaii) 4

Game 3–Lakeside (Northern California) 7, Legacy (Nevada) 1

Game 4–Lakeside (Northern California) 4, Arrowhead (Arizona) 1

Game 5–Legacy (Nevada) 10, Cedar American (Utah) 9

Game 6–Park View (Southern California) 15, Central East Maui (Hawaii) 2 (4 innings) (HRs–Garcia (2), Graft (2), Rios, Castro, Armenta, Godfrey)

Game 7–Lakeside (Northern California) 10, Cedar American (Utah) 0 (4 innings)

Game 8–Park View (Southern California) 20, Arrowhead (Arizona) 1 (4 innings) (HRs–Graft (2), Castro (2), Garcia)

Game 9–Central East Maui (Hawaii) 4, Cedar American (Utah) 0

Game 10–Park View (Southern California) 10, Legacy (Nevada) 5 (HRs–Rios, Ramirez, Garcia (2), Roberto, Armenta, Godfrey)

Game 11–Lakeside (Northern California) 5, Central East Maui (Hawaii) 3

Game 12–Legacy (Nevada) 12, Arrowhead (Arizona) 9 (7 innings)

Game 13–Park View (Southern California) 15, Legacy (Nevada) 2 (4 innings) (Eliminated) (HRs–Garcia (3), Graft, Armenta (2)

Game 14–Lakeside (Northern California) 9, Arrowhead (Arizona) 8 (Eliminated)

TITLE Game–Park View (Southern California) 11, Lakeside (Northern California) 4 (Eliminated) (HRs–Rios, Garcia (2), Ramirez)

Little League World Series (August 21 through August 30)

Host—Williamsport, Pennsylvania

United States Pool Play Game 1A–Mid-Atlantic 10, Northwest 2 (1 P.M. Volunteer Stadium)

Game 2A–Southeast 11, Midwest 3 (5 P.M. Volunteer Stadium)

Game 1B–Southwest 10, New England 1 (8 P.M. Lamade Stadium)

Game 3A–Southeast 6, Mid-Atlantic 3 (3 P.M. Lamade Stadium)

Game 2B–West 1, Great Lakes 0 (F/5) (8 P.M. Lamade Stadium–Attendance 19,500) (PVLL HRs–Ramirez (2), Roberto, Armenta, Godfrey, Rios, Garcia)

Game 4A–Midwest 5, Northwest 3 (12 P.M. Lamade Stadium)

Game 3B–Southwest 12, Great Lakes 0 (F/4) (2 P.M. Volunteer Stadium)

Game 4B–West 14, New England 0 (6 P.M. Volunteer Stadium–Attendance 10,200) (PVLL HRs–Rios (2), Godfrey)

Game 5A–Southeast 3, Northwest 2 (4 P.M. Lamade Stadium)

Game 6A–Mid-Atlantic 8, Midwest 3 (8 P.M. Lamade Stadium)

Game 5B–New England 12, Great Lakes 3 (4 P.M. Volunteer Stadium)

Game 6B–Southwest 6, West 3 (8 P.M. Lamade Stadium–Attendance 22,750) (PVLL HRs–Garcia)

Single Elimination Semifinals

International Game 1–Mexico 6, Japan 0 (Lamade Stadium)

USA Game 1–Southwest 4, Mid-Atlantic 1 (Eliminated) (Lamade Stadium)

International Game 2 –Asia-Pacific 5, Caribbean 2 (Eliminated) (Lamade Stadium)

USA Game 2–West 11, Southeast 10 (Eliminated) (Lamade Stadium–Attendance 21,000) (PVLL HRs–Godfrey, Ramirez, Garcia, Rios)

International TITLE Game–Asia-Pacific 9, Mexico 4 (Eliminated)
(Lamade Stadium)

**USA TITLE Game–West 12, Southwest 2 (Eliminated) (4 innings)
(Lamade Stadium–Attendance 13,400) (PVLL HRs–Ramirez,
Graft (2), Rios)**

Consolation Game–Mexico 5, Southwest 4 (Volunteer Stadium)

August 30, 2009–3 P.M. Lamade Stadium

**WORLD SERIES CHAMPIONSHIP GAME–(Lamade Stadium–
Attendance 32,400)**

West 6, Asia-Pacific 3 (PVLL HRs–none)

Sources

Unpublished Sources

Interviews

Armenta, Isaiah, Park View Little League All-Star player. Interviewed by authors, October 2009.

Castro, Oscar, Park View Little League All-Star manager. Interviewed by authors, October 2009 and March 2010.

Castro, Oscar, Park View Little League All-Star player. Interviewed by authors, October 2009.

Conlin, Jim, parent of Park View Little League All-Star player Nick Conlin. Interviewed by authors, October 2009.

Foggiano, Frank, 1961 El Cajon-La Mesa Northern Little League All-Star player. Interviewed by authors, October 2009.

Garcia, Shelly, Park View Little League board member. Interviewed by authors, October 2009.

Godfrey, Russell, parent of Park View Little League All-Star player Seth Godfrey. Interviewed by authors, October 2009.

Godfrey, Seth, Park View Little League All-Star player. Interviewed by authors, October 2009.

Graft, Cory and Pua, parents of Park View Little League All-Star player Bulla Graft. Interviewed by authors, October 2009.

McNaughton, Mike, Park View Little League board member. Interviewed by authors, November 2009.

Melin, Markus, Park View Little League All-Star player. Interviewed by authors, October 2009.

Peterson, Jensen, Park View Little League All-Star player. Interviewed by authors, November 2009.

Porras Jr., Daniel, Park View Little League All-Star player. Interviewed by authors, October 2009.

Ramirez, Kasey, parent of Park View Little League All-Star player Luke Ramirez. Interviewed by authors, October 2009.

Ramirez, Luke, Park View Little League All-Star player. Interviewed by authors, October 2009.

Ramirez, Ric, Park View Little League All-Star coach. Interviewed by authors, November 2009 and January 2010.

Rhylick, Brent, Rancho Santa Margarita All-Star coach. Interviewed by authors, January 2010.

Rios, Andy, parent of Park View Little League All-Star player Andy Rios. Interviewed by authors, April 2010.

Rios, Andy, Park View Little League All-Star player. Interviewed by authors, November 2009.

Roberto, Bradley, Park View Little League All-Star player. Interviewed by authors, October 2009.

Roberto, Rod, Park View Little League president. Interviewed by authors, October 2009.

Schneeman, Patrick, Sweetwater Valley Little League All-Star coach. Interviewed by authors, November 2009.

Vega, Danny, former Park View Little League coach. Interviewed by authors, November 2009.

Miscellany

E-mail from Chris Downs, Little League baseball and softball director of publicity, August 9, 2010.

E-mail from Randall Clark, September 1, 2009.

E-mail from Randy Atkinson, Oceanside American Little League All-Star coach, August 17, 2009.

E-mail from Rod Roberto, Park View Little League president, August 15, 2009.

E-mail from Sharon Garcia, parent of Park View Little League All-Star player Kiko Garcia, August 19, 2009.

E-mail from Steve Gottlieb, Torrance Little League president, August 18, 2009.

Flyer from Eastlake Church, August 2009.

Letter from Eastlake Little League board of directors, August 10, 2009.

Questionnaire completed by Andy Rios, Park View Little League All-Star player, March 2010.

Questionnaire completed by Bradley Roberto, Park View Little League All-Star player, March 2010.

Questionnaire completed by Bulla Graft, Park View Little League All-Star player, March 2010.

Questionnaire completed by Daniel Porras Jr., Park View Little League All-Star player, March 2010.

Questionnaire completed by Isaiah Armenta, Park View Little League All-Star player, March 2010.

Questionnaire completed by Jensen Peterson, Park View Little League All-Star player, April 2010.

Questionnaire completed by Kiko Garcia, Park View Little League All-Star player, April 2010.

Questionnaire completed by Luke Ramirez, Park View Little League All-Star player, March 2010.

Questionnaire completed by Markus Melin, Park View Little League All-Star player, March 2010.

Questionnaire completed by Nick Conlin, Park View Little League All-Star player, March 2010.

Questionnaire completed by Oscar Castro, Park View Little League All-Star player, April 2010.

Questionnaire completed by Seth Godfrey, Park View Little League All-Star player, March 2010.

Published Sources

Internet Resources

10news.com

active.com

associatedcontent.com

baseball-almanac.com

baseball-reference.com

beachcalifornia.com

cfll-north.com/for-our-coaches

ci.chula-vista.ca.us

dailybulletin.com

dailynews.com

eteamz.active.com
factfinder.census.gov
gov.ca.gov
littleleague.org
nbcsandiego.com
sdnn.com
signonsandiego.com
southwilliamsport.net
sports.espn.go.com
sportsvideo.org
sungazette.com
ucsdtritons.com.
unpage.org
voiceofsandiego.org

Books

Grisamore, Ed. *It Can Be Done: The Billy Henderson Story.* Henchard Press, Ltd., 2005.

Roseman, Frank M., and Peter J. Watry Jr. *Chula Vista.* Arcadia Publishing, 2008.

Periodical

The Sporting News

Film

Field of Dreams, Phil Alden Robinson, 1989.

Notes

Prologue

1. Quotation popularly attributed to Yogi Berra without specific citation.
2. www.littleleague.org/learn/about/historyandmission.htm.
3. www.littleleague.org/media/newsarchive/2009/May-Aug/2009LLBBWest.htm.
4. active.typepad.com/teamsports/2007/01/being_a_good_sp.html.
5. www.littleleague.org/learn/about/historyandmission.htm.
6. sportsvideo.org/main/blog/2009/09/03/little-league-world-series-big-ratings-for-espn-espn2-abc/.
7. www3.signonsandiego.com/news/2009/aug/26/n79492202455-park-view-players-stay-loose-focused/.
8. Interview with Rod Roberto, Park View Little League president, October 2009.

Chapter 1

1. *Field of Dreams,* Phil Alden Robinson, 1989.
2. Interview with Oscar Castro, Park View Little League All-Star player, October 2009.
3. Interview with Luke Ramirez, Park View Little League All-Star player, October 2009.
4. Interview with Bradley Roberto, Park View Little League All-Star player, October 2009.

5. Interview with Daniel Porras Jr., Park View Little League All-Star player, October 2009.

6. Interview with Seth Godfrey, Park View Little League All-Star player, October 2009.

7. Interview with Isaiah Armenta, Park View Little League All-Star player, October 2009.

8. Interview with Markus Melin, Park View Little League All-Star player, October 2009.

9. Interview with Kasey Ramirez, parent of Park View Little League All-Star player Luke Ramirez, October 2009.

10. Ibid.

11. Interview with Jim Conlin, parent of Park View Little League All-Star player Nick Conlin, October 2009.

12. Interview with Russell Godfrey, parent of Park View Little League All-Star player Seth Godfrey, October 2009.

13. Interview with Cory and Pua Graft, parents of Park View Little League All-Star player Bulla Graft, October 2009.

14. Interview with Oscar Castro, Park View Little League All-Star manager, October 2009.

15. Interview with Shelly Garcia, Park View Little League board member, October 2009.

Chapter 2

1. Quotation popularly attributed to Sparky Anderson without specific citation.

2. Interview with Andy Rios, Park View Little League All-Star player, November 2009, and questionnaire completed by Rios, March 2010.

3. Questionnaire completed by Kiko Garcia, April 2010.

4. Interview with Luke Ramirez, Park View Little League All-Star player, October 2009, and questionnaire completed by Ramirez, March 2010.

5. Interview with Cory and Pua Graft, parents of Park View Little League All-Star player Bulla Graft, October 2009, and questionnaire completed by Bulla Graft, March 2010.

6. Interview with Bradley Roberto, Park View Little League All-Star player, October 2009, and questionnaire completed by Roberto, March 2010.

7. Interview with Oscar Castro, Park View Little League All-Star player, October 2009, and questionnaire completed by Castro, April 2010.

8. Interview with Daniel Porras Jr., Park View Little League All-Star player, October 2009, and questionnaire completed by Porras Jr., March 2010.

9. Interview with Isaiah Armenta, Park View Little League All-Star player, October 2009, and questionnaire completed by Armenta, March 2010.

10. Interview with Markus Melin, Park View Little League All-Star player, October 2009, and questionnaire completed by Melin, March 2010.

11. Interview with Jim Conlin, parent of Park View Little League All-Star player Nick Conlin, October 2009, and questionnaire completed by Nick Conlin, March 2010.

12. Interview with Seth Godfrey, Park View Little League All-Star player, October 2009, and questionnaire completed by Godfrey, March 2010.

13. Interview with Jensen Peterson, Park View Little League All-Star player, November 2009, and questionnaire completed by Peterson, April 2010.

Chapter 3

1. Quotation popularly attributed to Babe Ruth without specific citation.

2. www.littleleague.org/learn/about/historyandmission.htm.

3. Ibid.

4. www.littleleague.org/learn/about/historyandmission/aroundtheworld. htm.

5. www.littleleague.org/learn/about/historyandmission/chronology.htm.

6. www.littleleague.org/learn/about/historyandmission/aroundtheworld. htm.

7. www.littleleague.org/media/newsarchive/2008stories/Little_League_ International_Mourns_the_Passing_of_Former_ABC__Wide_World_ of_Sports__Host_Jim_McKay_-_June_9.htm.

8. www.littleleague.org/learn/about/historyandmission/chronology.htm.

9. www.baseball-almanac.com/legendary/little_league_world_series_ major_league_world_series.shtml.

10. www.littleleague.org/learn/about/historyandmission/chronology.htm.

11. www.littleleague.org/learn/about/historyandmission/aroundtheworld. htm.

12. www.littleleague.org/learn/about/historyandmission/chronology.htm.

13. www.littleleague.org/learn/about/historyandmission/aroundtheworld.htm.

14. www.littleleague.org/learn/about/historyandmission/chronology.htm.

15. Ibid.

16. www.littleleague.org/media/newsarchive/03_2006/06famousvisitors.htm.

17. www.littleleague.org/learn/about/historyandmission/aroundtheworld.htm.

18. www.littleleague.org/learn/about/historyandmission/chronology.htm.

19. Ibid.

20. Ibid.

21. www.littleleague.org/learn/about/historyandmission/aroundtheworld.htm.

22. www.littleleague.org/learn/about/historyandmission.htm.

23. www.littleleague.org/learn/about/historyandmission/aroundtheworld.htm.

24. www.sdnn.com/sandiego/2009-08-18/sports/local-little-leaguers-recall-61-world-series-win.

25. Ibid.

26. Ibid.

27. Ibid.

28. Ibid.

29. Ibid.

30. Ibid.

31. Interview with Frank Foggiano, 1961 El Cajon-La Mesa Northern Little League All-Star player, October 2009.

32. Ibid.

33. www.littleleague.org/learn/about/historyandmission/chronology.htm.

34. www.beachcalifornia.com/san-diego-county-population.html.

35. www.associatedcontent.com/article/2975954/largest_cities_in_california_pg5.html?cat=4.

36. *Chula Vista,* by Frank M. Roseman and Peter J. Watry Jr., page 14.

37. factfinder.census.gov/servlet/STTable?_bm=y&-geo_id=
    16000US0613392&-qr_name=ACS_2008_3YR_G00_
    S0101&-ds_name=ACS_2008_3YR_G00_.

38. Roseman and Watry Jr., page 8.

39. http://www.ci.chula-vista.ca.us/city_services/community_services/
    library/LocalHistoryMuseum/LocalHistRmHistOfCV.asp.

40. Ibid.

41. Ibid.

42. Roseman and Watry Jr., page 106.

43. Interview with Danny Vega, former Park View Little League coach,
    November 2009.

44. Ibid.

45. Ibid.

46. Ibid.

47. Ibid.

48. Ibid.

49. Interview with Mike McNaughton, Park View Little League board
    member, November 2009.

50. Ibid.

51. Ibid.

52. Interview with Danny Vega, former Park View Little League coach,
    November 2009.

53. mlb.mlb.com/team/player.jsp?player_id=120747.

54. Interview with Rod Roberto, Park View Little League president,
    October 2009.

Chapter 4

1. Quotation popularly attributed to Branch Rickey without specific
   citation.

2. Interview with Rod Roberto, Park View Little League president,
   October 2009.

3. Ibid.

4. Ibid.

5. Ibid.

6. Ibid.

7. Ibid.

8. Ibid.

9. Interview with Ric Ramirez, Park View Little League All-Star coach, November 2009.

10. Interview with Rod Roberto, Park View Little League president, October 2009.

11. Ibid.

12. Interview with Brent Rhylick, Rancho Santa Margarita All-Star coach, January 2010.

13. Interview with Rod Roberto, Park View Little League president, October 2009.

14. Ibid.

15. Interview with Mike McNaughton, Park View Little League board member, November 2009.

16. Ibid.

17. Ibid.

18. Interview with Ric Ramirez, Park View Little League All-Star coach, November 2009.

19. Interview with Rod Roberto, Park View Little League president, October 2009.

20. Ibid.

21. Interview with Bradley Roberto, Park View Little League All-Star player, October 2009.

22. Interview with Oscar Castro, Park View Little League All-Star manager, October 2009.

23. Interview with Ric Ramirez, Park View Little League All-Star coach, November 2009.

24. Ibid.

25. Interview with Oscar Castro, Park View Little League All-Star manager, October 2009.

26. Interview with Rod Roberto, Park View Little League president, October 2009.

27. Ibid.

28. Ibid.

29. Interview with Ric Ramirez, Park View Little League All-Star coach, November 2009.

30. Interview with Rod Roberto, Park View Little League president, October 2009.

31. Interview with Brent Rhylick, Rancho Santa Margarita All-Star coach, January 2010.

32. Interview with Ric Ramirez, Park View Little League All-Star coach, January 2010.

33. Ibid.

34. Interview with Rod Roberto, Park View Little League president, October 2009.

35. sports.espn.go.com/espn/eticket/story?page=cerda.

36. Ibid.

37. Interview with Rod Roberto, Park View Little League president, October 2009.

38. Interview with Brent Rhylick, Rancho Santa Margarita All-Star coach, January 2010.

Chapter 5

1. Quotation popularly attributed to Willie Mays without specific citation.

2. www.littleleague.org/managersandcoaches/coachrole.htm.

3. www.cfll-north.com/for-our-coaches.

4. Interview with Ric Ramirez, Park View Little League All-Star coach, November 2009.

5. Ibid.

6. www.ucsdtritons.com/ViewArticle. dbml?DB_OEM_ID=5800&ATCLID=204778647.

7. Interview with Ric Ramirez, Park View Little League All-Star coach, November 2009.

8. Interview with Oscar Castro, Park View Little League All-Star manager, October 2009.

9. Ibid.

10. Ibid.

11. Ibid.

12. Interview with Jensen Peterson, Park View Little League All-Star player, November 2009.

13. Interview with Andy Rios, Park View Little League All-Star player, November 2009.

14. Interview with Oscar Castro, Park View Little League All-Star manager, October 2009.

15. Ibid.

16. Ibid.

17. Interview with Cory and Pua Graft, parents of Park View Little League All-Star player Bulla Graft, October 2009.

18. Interview with Ric Ramirez, Park View Little League All-Star coach, January 2010.

19. Interview with Ric Ramirez, Park View Little League All-Star coach, November 2009.

20. Ibid.

21. Interview with Brent Rhylick, Rancho Santa Margarita All-Star coach, January 2010.

22. Ibid.

23. Interview with Ric Ramirez, Park View Little League All-Star coach, January 2010.

24. www3.signonsandiego.com/news/2009/aug/27/park-view-players-stay-loose-focused/.

25. Interview with Oscar Castro, Park View Little League All-Star manager, October 2009.

26. Interview with Ric Ramirez, Park View Little League All-Star coach, January 2010.

27. Ibid.

28. Ibid.

29. Ibid.

30. Interview with Oscar Castro, Park View Little League All-Star manager, October 2009.

Chapter 6

1. Quotation popularly attributed to Babe Ruth without specific citation.

2. Interview with Rod Roberto, Park View Little League president, October 2009.

3. www.littleleague.org/Assets/forms_pubs/tournaments/TournRules_BB.pdf.

4. Ibid.

5. Interview with Ric Ramirez, Park View Little League All-Star coach, January 2010.

6. www.signonsandiego.com/news/2009/aug/20/big-friendly-giant/?metro.

7. Interview with Ric Ramirez, Park View Little League All-Star coach, January 2010.

8. Interview with Andy Rios, parent of Park View Little League All-Star player Andy Rios, April 2010.

9. Interview with Patrick Schneeman, Sweetwater Valley Little League All-Star coach, November 2009.

10. Ibid.

11. Ibid.

12. www.littleleague.org/Assets/forms_pubs/media/PitchingRegulation-Changes_BB_11-13-09.pdf.

13. Interview with Ric Ramirez, Park View Little League All-Star coach, January 2010.

14. Ibid.

15. Ibid.

16. Interview with Patrick Schneeman, Sweetwater Valley Little League All-Star coach, November 2009.

17. Ibid.

18. Ibid.

Chapter 7

1. *The Sporting News*, May 12, 1970.

2. www.littleleague.org/learn/about/structure.htm.

3. www.unpage.org/shared/un-genin.htm.

4. Ibid.

5. www.unpage.org/nocal/.

6. www.unpage.org/socal/.

7. Ibid.

8. www.unpage.org/nocal/.

9. eteamz.active.com/llbwest/files/HistoryOfTheWesternRegion1.pdf.

10. www.littleleague.org/series/2009divisions/llbb/series.htm.

11. Interview with Daniel Porras Jr., Park View Little League All-Star player, October 2009.

12. Interview with Brent Rhylick, Rancho Santa Margarita All-Star coach, January 2010.

13. www.littleleague.org/Assets/forms_pubs/media/PitchingRegulation-Changes_BB_11-13-09.pdf.

14. Interview with Ric Ramirez, Park View Little League All-Star coach, January 2010.

15. Interview with Ric Ramirez, Park View Little League All-Star coach, November 2010.

16. Ibid.

17. Interview with Ric Ramirez, Park View Little League All-Star coach, January 2010.

18. Interview with Brent Rhylick, Rancho Santa Margarita All-Star coach, January 2010.

19. Ibid.

20. Ibid.

Chapter 8

1. Quotation popularly attributed to Christy Mathewson without specific citation.

2. Interview with Brent Rhylick, Rancho Santa Margarita All-Star coach, January 2010.

3. Ibid.

4. Interview with Oscar Castro, Park View Little League All-Star manager, October 2009.

5. Ibid.

6. Interview with Patrick Schneeman, Sweetwater Valley Little League All-Star coach, November 2009.

7. Interview with Oscar Castro, Park View Little League All-Star manager, October 2009.

8. Interview with Ric Ramirez, Park View Little League All-Star coach, January 2010.

9. Ibid.

10. www.dailynews.com/sports/ci_12981028?source=rss.

11. Interview with Patrick Schneeman, Sweetwater Valley Little League All-Star coach, November 2009.

12. www.dailybreeze.com/ci_12977304.

13. Interview with Andy Rios, parent of Park View Little League All-Star player Andy Rios, April 2010.

14. www.dailynews.com/sports/ci_12981028?source=rss.

15. www.dailybreeze.com/preps/ci_12988145.

16. Ibid.

17. Interview with Rod Roberto, Park View Little League president, October 2009.

18. Interview with Ric Ramirez, Park View Little League All-Star coach, January 2010.

19. Interview with Patrick Schneeman, Sweetwater Valley Little League All-Star coach, November 2009.

20. Letter from Eastlake Little League board of directors, August 10, 2009.

Chapter 9

1. Quotation popularly attributed to Dave Bristol without specific citation.

2. www.dailybulletin.com/ci_13002616.

3. Interview with Cory and Pua Graft, parents of Park View Little League All-Star player Bulla Graft, October 2009.

4. Interview with Jim Conlin, parent of Park View Little League All-Star player Nick Conlin.

5. Interview with Rod Roberto, Park View Little League president, October 2009.

6. Interview with Ric Ramirez, Park View Little League All-Star coach, November 2009.

7. www.littleleague.org/series/2009divisions/llbb/BoxScores/WS02.html.

8. www.littleleague.org/series/2009divisions/llbb/BoxScores/WS12. html.

9. Interview with Ric Ramirez, Park View Little League All-Star coach, January 2010.

10. Ibid.

11. Interview with Oscar Castro, Park View Little League All-Star manager, October 2009.

12. www.littleleague.org/series/2009divisions/llbb/BoxScores/WS16. html.

13. www.littleleague.org/series/2009divisions/llbb/BoxScores/WS20. html.

14. www.littleleague.org/series/2009divisions/llbb/BoxScores/WSsf01. html.

15. Flyer from Eastlake Church, August 2009.

16. www.littleleague.org/series/2009divisions/llbb/BoxScores/WSCH. html.

17. www.dailybulletin.com/littleleague/ci_13142038.

18. Ibid.

19. Ibid.

20. E-mail from Rod Roberto, Park View Little League president, August 15, 2009.

21. E-mail from Randy Atkinson, Oceanside American Little League All-Star coach, August 17, 2009.

22. E-mail from Steve Gottlieb, Torrance Little League president, August 18, 2009.

23. Interview with Patrick Schneeman, Sweetwater Valley Little League All-Star coach, November 2009.

24. Interview with Brent Rhylick, Rancho Santa Margarita All-Star coach, January 2010.

25. www.signonsandiego.com/news/2009/aug/21/1s21little2318-official-park-view-home-runs-are-le/.

26. Ibid.

27. Ibid.

28. Ibid.

29. Ibid.

Chapter 10

1. Quotation popularly attributed to Walt Alston without specific citation.

2. www.signonsandiego.com/news/2009/aug/18/little-leaguers-families-seek-travel-aid/?metro&zIndex=151139.

3. www.signonsandiego.com/news/2009/aug/18/journey-pa-begins-first-flights-fame/.

4. www.signonsandiego.com/news/2009/aug/18/journey-pa-begins-first-flights-fame/.

5. www.signonsandiego.com/news/2009/aug/18/little-leaguers-families-seek-travel-aid/?metro&zIndex=151139.

6. www.signonsandiego.com/news/2009/aug/18/journey-pa-begins-first-flights-fame/.

7. Interview with Oscar Castro, Park View Little League All-Star player, October 2009.

8. Interview with Oscar Castro, Park View Little League All-Star manager, March 2010.

9. E-mail from Sharon Garcia, parent of Park View Little League All-Star player Kiko Garcia, August 19, 2009.

10. Ibid.

11. Interview with Oscar Castro, Park View Little League All-Star player, October 2009.

12. Interview with Luke Ramirez, Park View Little League All-Star player, October 2009.

13. E-mail from Chris Downs, Director of Publicity, Little League Baseball, August 9, 2010.

14. www.southwilliamsport.net/borough_main.htm.

15. www.sdnn.com/sandiego/2009-08-21/blog/americas-finest-sports-blog/live-from-williamsport-with-park-view-little-league.

16. Interview with Ric Ramirez, Park View Little League All-Star coach, January 2010.

17. www.littleleague.org/series/2009divisions/llbb/WSBoxScores/LLWS09.html.

18. www.baseball-reference.com/teams/PIT/2009-schedule-scores.shtml.

19. www.littleleague.org/series/2009divisions/llbb/
gamestories/22Saturday/game9/gamestory_template.html.

20. www.littleleague.org/learn/about/historyandmission/chronology.
htm.

21. www.littleleague.org/series/2009divisions/llbb/WSBoxScores/
LLWS13.html.

22. www.signonsandiego.com/news/2009/aug/24/1s24little232437-boys-
breathe-sigh-relief-pitch-co/?sports&zIndex=154316.

23. www.littleleague.org/series/2009divisions/llbb/WSBoxScores/
LLWS24.html.

24. www.littleleague.org/series/2009divisions/llbb/
gamestories/25Tuesday/game24/gamestory _template.html.

25. Interview with Oscar Castro, Park View Little League All-Star manager, October 2009.

26. Interview with Kasey Ramirez, parent of Park View Little League All-
Star player Luke Ramirez, October 2009.

27. Ibid.

28. Interview with Ric Ramirez, Park View Little League All-Star coach,
January 2010.

29. Ibid.

30. *It Can Be Done: The Billy Henderson Story,* by Ed Grisamore, page 13.

31. www.littleleague.org/series/2007divisions/llbb/
gamestories/26sunday/game32/gamestory.htm.

32. Interview with Oscar Castro, Park View Little League All-Star manager, October 2009.

33. www.littleleague.org/series/2009divisions/llbb/
gamestories/27Thursday/game28/gamestory _template.html.

34. www.littleleague.org/series/2009divisions/llbb/WSBoxScores/
LLWS28.html.

35. www.sungazette.com/page/content.detail/id/531611.html?nav=5156.

36. Interview with Rod Roberto, Park View Little League president,
October 2009.

37. www.signonsandiego.com/news/2009/aug/29/bn29little175846/.

38. Ibid.

39. www.littleleague.org/series/2009divisions/llbb/gamestories/
30Sunday/game32/gamestory _notes.html.

40. www.littleleague.org/series/2009divisions/llbb/WSBoxScores/ LLWS32.html.

41. Interview with Ric Ramirez, Park View Little League All-Star coach, January 2010.

42. www.littleleague.org/series/2009divisions/llbb/ gamestories/30Sunday/game32/gamestory_ template.html.

43. Ibid.

44. Ibid.

45. Ibid.

46. Interview with Oscar Castro, Park View Little League All-Star manager, October 2009.

Epilogue

1. Quotation popularly attributed to Babe Ruth without specific citation.

2. E-mail from Randall Clark, September 1, 2009.

3. gov.ca.gov/press-release/13097/.

4. www.nbcsandiego.com/news/sports/Chula-Vista-Champs-Come-Home-56413492.html?__source=Facebook5.

5. www.signonsandiego.com/news/2009/sep/01/boys-get-big-league-welcome/.

6. Ibid.

7. www.10news.com/news/20676675/detail.html.

8. Ibid.

9. Ibid.

10. Ibid.

11. www.10news.com/news/20722367/detail.html.

12. Interview with Oscar Castro, Park View Little League All-Star player, October 2009.

13. Interview with Luke Ramirez, Park View Little League All-Star player, October 2009.

14. Interview with Bradley Roberto, Park View Little League All-Star player, October 2009.

15. Interview with Daniel Porras, Park View Little League All-Star player, October 2009.

16. Interview with Seth Godfrey, Park View Little League All-Star player, October 2009.

17. Interview with Isaiah Armenta, Park View Little League All-Star player, October 2009.

18. Interview with Markus Melin, Park View Little League All-Star player, October 2009.

19. Interview with Jensen Peterson, Park View Little League All-Star player, November 2009.

20. Interview with Luke Ramirez, Park View Little League All-Star player, October 2009.

21. Interview with Kasey Ramirez, parent of Park View Little League All-Star player Luke Ramirez, October 2009.

22. Questionnaire completed by Isaiah Armenta, Park View Little League All-Star player, March 2010.

23. Interview with Jim Conlin, parent of Park View Little League All-Star player Nick Conlin.

24. Interview with Markus Melin, Park View Little League All-Star player, October 2009.

Appendix

1. Compiled from www.littleleague.org and www.unpage.org.

Index

A

Al Houghton Stadium, 74

Allen, Mel, 23

Almonte, Danny, 41, 55

Almonte, Felipe, 41

Alworth, Lance, 7

Anderson, Sparky, 8

Arizona team (Arrowhead Little League), 74, 78, 79

Armenta, Isaiah, vii, x, 4, 10, 11, 33, 39, 40, 41, 54, 104, 105

  bio, 16

  District 42 Tournament, 58

  divisional tournament, 69, 71

  Little League World Series, 87, 92, 95, 98, 110

  Section 7 Tournament, 62, 108

  subdivisional tournament, 65

  West Regional Tournament, 76, 77, 78, 79, 80, 81, 82, 109

Aros, David, 68

Arrowhead Little League (Arizona), 74, 78, 79

Asia-Pacific Taoyuan. *See* Chinese Taipei

Atkinson, Randy, 82

B

Baranowski, Kathy, ix

Bats

  aluminum, 25

  doctoring accusation, 84

Bench, Johnny, 23

Berra, Yogi, xiii

Big Red Machine (Torrance), 71

Blue Bombers. *See* Park View Blue Bombers

Boggs, Wade, 22

Bospflug, Rena, 30

Brawley, California, 62

Breitbard Hall of Fame, 7, 106

Brett, George, 22

Briare, Connor, 81

Bristol, Dave, 74

Brooks, Drew, 94

Broughton, Cortez, 54

Bryant, Kobe, 104

Byers, Patty, 28

Byers, Randy, 28

C

Cargin, Rodger, 24

Carlton, Steve, 22

Carter, Gary, 22

Castro, Oscar, Jr., vii, x, 2, 34, 39, 54, 103

  bio, 14

  District 42 Tournament, 59, 108

  divisional tournament, 71

  Little League World Series, 93, 95–96

  Section 7 Tournament, 62

  West Regional Tournament, 76, 77, 78, 81, 109

Castro, Oscar, Sr., vii, x, xiv, 6, 14, 34,
  37–38, 39, 53, 106
  bio, 45–46
  coaching philosophy of, 46–52
  District 42 Tournament, 56, 57
  divisional tournament, 68, 69–70, 72–73
  Little League World Series, 88, 89, 93, 94,
    95, 97, 100
  responsibilities of, 43–45
  subdivisional tournament, 64–65
  West Regional Tournament, 75, 76, 77,
    78, 79, 82, 84
Cedar American Little League, 74
Central East Maui Little League (Hawaii),
  74, 76–77
Chadwick, Florence, 7
Chandler, Bob, 104
Chinese Taipei, xv, 1, 23, 55, 91, 98–99
Chintala, Tom, ix
Chula Vista, California, 26–27, 31
Clairemont Hilltoppers, 63
Coaches
  eligibility requirements of, 43
  expectations for, 43–44
  of Park View, 43–52
Conditioning, 50
Conlin, Jim, 5, 75, 106
Conlin, Nick, vii, x, 5, 16, 34
  bio, 18
  Little League World Series, 93, 96, 99
Connolly, Maureen "Little Mo," 7
Corona National team, 64
Correale, Matt, 93
Cosell, Howard, 22
Cox, Cheryl, 102

D
Daves, Travis, 94
District 42 Tournament, 53–59
  recap, 107–108
Divisional Championship Tournament,
  67–73
  recap, 109
Dorado, Jaime, viii
Double elimination tournament, defined,
  60
Drysdale, Don, 23
Durley, Cameron, 55

E
Eastlake Church, 80
Eastlake Little League, 30, 73
Edrozo, Angie, 28
Edrozo, Bill, 28, 29
El Cajon, California, 23, 31, 98
El Campo, Texas, 98
Encino Little League, 67

F
Fingers, Rollie, 22
Fisk, Carlton, 23
Fletcher Hills Little League, 31
Foggiano, Frank, 25
Ford, Andrew, x
Ford, Anne, ix, x
Ford, Carolyn, ix, x
Ford, Daniel, x
Ford, Elizabeth, x
Fundamentals, 50–51
Fundraising for the Little League World
  Series, 86–87

G
Garcia, Kiko, vii, x, 11, 33, 39, 40, 54
  bio, 10
  District 42 Tournament, 55, 57, 107
  divisional tournament, 69, 71, 109
  Little League World Series, 92, 93–94, 95,
    98, 99, 100, 110, 111
  Section 7 Tournament, 62, 63, 108
  subdivisional tournament, 65, 66,
    108
  West Regional Tournament, 76, 77, 78,
    79, 80, 81, 109, 110
Garcia, Sharon, x, 75, 88–89
Garcia, Shelly, viii, 6–7
Garfinkel, Tom, iii
Georgia team (Warner Robins Little
  League), 50, 91, 94, 95, 96–97
Gershow, Ira, ix
Gerstenslager, Jim, 84
Gibson, Bob, 23
Godfrey, Russell, viii, 3, 5, 19
Godfrey, Seth, vii, x, 3–4, 5, 33, 34, 104
  bio, 19
  District 42 Tournament, 107
  divisional tournament, 72, 73, 109

Little League World Series, 92, 93, 99, 110, 111
  Section 7 Tournament, 62, 108
  subdivisional tournament, 66, 108
  West Regional Tournament, 77, 79, 109
Gonzales, Adrian, 4, 103
Gorillas, 34, 40, 56
Gottlieb, Steve, 83
Gowdy, Curt, 23
Grady, Robin, 28
Grady, Walt, 28
Graft, Bulla, vii, x, 3, 6, 33, 34, 54
  bio, 12
  District 42 Tournament, 107, 108
  Little League World Series, 95, 97, 99, 111
  Section 7 Tournament, 62, 63, 108
  subdivisional tournament, 65, 66, 108
  West Regional Tournament, 76, 77, 78, 81, 109
Graft, Cory, 6, 33, 34, 48, 75
Graft, Pua, 6, 48
Grand Slam Parade, 90
Granite Bay team, West Regional Tournament, 80–81
Green Machine
  name origin, 60
  transition to Blue Bombers, 92
Gwynn, Tony, 7, 23, 104

H
Hall of Champions, San Diego, 1–2, 7, 106
Hart, Mitch, 81
Hawaii team (Central East Maui Little League), 74, 76–77
Hayward, Alan, 30
Hershiser, Orel, 23
Hosman, Matt, 93
Hunter, Jim "Catfish", 22

I
Imperial Beach team, 55
Imperial County team, 62
Inzunza, Jonalee, viii

J
Jay, Joey, 22
Jones, Randy, 7, 96, 103

K
Kirkland, Washington, 23

L
Laguna Hills team, 63
Lakeside Little League, 74, 80–81
Lamade Stadium, 3, 23, 91, 92, 93, 98
La Mesa Little League, 30–31
La Mesa Northern All-Stars, 23–26, 97
Legacy Little League (Nevada), 74, 79, 80
Lemon Grove, California, 60, 62
Leonard, Chico, 24
Levittown, Pennsylvania, 24
Lewis, Claude, 95
Lindenberger, Kayoko, ix, x
Lindenberger, Max, x
Lindenberger, Paula, x
Little League
  charter, 23
  coaches of, 43–44
  eligibility requirements of, 54–55
  story of, 21–31
Little League World Series, ix, xiii–xiv, 1
  1961, 23–26
  2009, 86–100
  aftermath of, 101–106
  dormitories at, 88–89
  first, 22
  perfect game in, 41, 97
  preparation for, 82, 86–87
  recap, 110–111
  televised, 22–23, 25, 26, 87, 91, 93, 98
  tournaments that precede, 60–62
  travel to, 87–88
  uncles assigned to teams at, 88
Littler, Gene, 7
Logan County/Russellville Little League, 91–92
Lopez, George, iii, 1, 102, 104
Lopez-Zepeda, Elva, viii
Lucero, Ernie, 54
Luckie Waller Little League, 55

M
Macias, Angel, 41, 97
Main, Korrin, ix
Malkoff, Scott, ix
Mantle, Mickey, 23

Maris, Roger, 23
Marmolejo, Alex, vii
Marmolejo, Hope, viii
Mathewson, Christy, 67
Maynard Midgets, 22
Mays, Willie, 43
McAllister Park American Little League
    (Texas), 91, 93–94
McCord, Matt, 81
McKay, Jim, 22, 23
McNaughton, Mike, viii, x, 29, 30, 36
Melia, Terry, ix
Melin, Markus, vii, x, 4, 16, 33, 34, 104, 106
    bio, 17
    District 42 Tournament, 58
    Little League World Series, 87
Michaels, Al, 23
Mission Trails team, 66
Mitchell, Jane, ix–x, 104–105
Monterrey Industrial Little League
    (Mexico), 97–98
Monterrey team (1957), 22
Moorad, Jeff, 86
Moore, Archie, 7
Mother Goose Parade, El Cajon, California,
    104
Musashi-Fuchu Little League, 92, 97
Musberger, Brent, 23, 98
Myers, Steve, viii

N

Nevada team (Legacy Little League), 74, 79, 80
Nevin, Phil, 103
Norcross, Don, 83
Northern El Cajon, California, 98
Norton, Jeff, viii
Norton, Ken, 7

O

Obama, Barack, 104
O'Brien, Conan, 103
Olloque, Manny, Jr., 68, 70, 71, 72
Ou, Chin, 98, 99

P

Palmer, Jim, 22, 23
Park View Blue Bombers, ix, xi–xii
    2007 and 2008 seasons, 38–39

2009 season, 39–42
    compared to La Mesa, 24–26
    from Green Machine to, 92
    nickname origin, xiii, xv
    roster, 2009, vii
    team bios, 8–20
Park View Little League, ix, xi–xii, xiii–xv
    history of, 27–31
Paznokas, Nancy, ix
Peabody Western Little League, 92–93
Perfect Game, The, 22, 98
Peterson, Jensen, vii, x, 34, 47, 104
    bio, 20
    District 42 Tournament, 59, 107, 108
    Little League World Series, 99
    West Regional Tournament, 76, 109
Pitching, rules about, 57, 64
Pool play tournament, defined, 61
Porras, Daniel "Junior," vii, x, 3, 33, 34, 50,
    103
    bio, 15
    Little League World Series, 93, 95–96
    Section 7 Tournament, 62, 108
    subdivisional tournament, 63
Pratt, Todd, 30

R

Ramirez, Ben, 46
Ramirez, Kasey, 4–5, 36, 54, 94, 105
Ramirez, Luke, vii, x, xiv, 2, 4, 10, 19, 34,
    39, 46, 49, 103, 105
    bio, 11
    District 42 Tournament, 55, 57–59,
    107
    divisional tournament, 68, 71, 72, 109
    eligibility questions about, 54–55
    Little League World Series, 88–89, 91, 92,
    95, 97, 100, 110, 111
    Section 7 Tournament, 62, 63, 108
    subdivisional tournament, 65–66, 108
    West Regional Tournament, 76, 79, 81,
    109, 110
Ramirez, Ric, vii, x, xiv, 2, 4, 6, 11, 20, 34,
    36–38, 39, 40, 53, 106
    bio, 46
    coaching philosophy of, 47–52
    District 42 Tournament, 56, 57, 58
    divisional tournament, 69–70, 72–73

Little League World Series, 88, 89, 91, 93, 95
   responsibilities of, 43–45
   subdivisional tournament, 64–66
   West Regional Tournament, 75, 76, 77, 78, 84
Rancho San Diego Little League, 62
Rancho Santa Margarita Little League, xv, 5, 35, 38–42
   subdivisional tournament, 49, 63–66
Reck, Chris, 39, 64
Respect the game theme, 49
Rhodes, Don, 30
Rhodes, Karen, 30
Rhylick, Brent, x, 35, 42, 49, 64, 66, 67, 83
Rhylick, Matthew, 39, 64, 66
Rickey, Branch, 32
Rios, Andy, Jr., vii, x, 4, 11, 15, 33, 34, 47, 51, 65
   bio, 9
   District 42 Tournament, 57, 107, 108
   divisional tournament, 72, 109
   Little League World Series, 92, 93, 95, 96, 97, 99, 100, 110, 111
   Section 7 Tournament, 62, 63, 108
   subdivisional tournament, 108
   West Regional Tournament, 77, 79, 81, 109, 110
Rios, Andy, Sr., x
Roberto, Austin, 13, 32
Roberto, Bradley, vii, x, 3, 19, 32, 33, 34, 37, 103
   bio, 13
   divisional tournament, 72, 109
   Little League World Series, 92, 110
   subdivisional tournament, 108
   West Regional Tournament, 79, 81, 109
Roberto, Cody, 13, 32
Roberto, Rod, vii, x, xiv, 1, 2, 6, 13, 31, 41, 53, 66, 72, 73, 82, 90, 96
   strategy of, 32–38
Robinson, Brooks, 23
Robinson, Jackie, 23
Rojas, Danny Almonte, 41
Rose Bowl Parade, 104
Ruth, Babe, 21, 23, 53, 101
Ryan, Nolan, 22

S
Salvatore, Michael, 24
San Diego Chargers, Blue Bombers meet, 102–103
San Diego Hall of Champions Sports Museum, 1–2, 7, 106
Schenkel, Chris, 23
Schmidt, Mike, 22
Schneeman, Daniel, 56, 57
Schneeman, Patrick, x, 56–57, 58, 59, 69, 73, 83
Schwarzenegger, Arnold, 102
Seaver, Tom, 22
Section 7 Tournament, 60–63
   recap, 108
Shull, Mike, 94
Sipe, Brian, iii, 7, 24
Smith, Billy Ray, iii, xii, 104
Smith, Conner, 96
South Bay Little League, 4, 34
Southwestern College stadium, celebration at, 102, 103
South Williamsport, Pennsylvania, 22
Stargell, Willie, 23
Stotz, Carl, 21–22
Subdivisional tournament, 63–66
   recap, 108
Sung, Wen Hua, 98
Sutton, Don, 22
Sweetwater Valley Little League, 30, 53, 55–59
Sycuan Tribal Group, donation by, 86

T
T-ball, inventor of, 95
Team Soar, 34
Texas team (McAllister Park American Little League), 91, 93–94
Thomas, Calin, 84
Three C's theme, 48–49
Tomlinson, LaDainian, 102
Tonight Show with Conan O'Brien, 103
Torio, Brandon, 57
Torrance Little League, 67–73
Tournaments
   double elimination, defined, 60
   levels of, 60–62
   pool play, defined, 61
Tuyay, Jim, 32

U

Uecker, Bob, 23
Upland Foothill team, 64
Utah team, West Regional Tournament,
74, 76

V

Vega, Danny, x, 27–28, 29, 30
Vega, Javy, 40–41
Vega, José, 40
Vega, Sal, 96
Volunteer Stadium, 92

W

Walton, Bill, 2
Wanamaker, Mike, 34
Warmkessel, Jerry, viii
Warner Robins Little League (Georgia), 50,
91, 94, 95, 96–97
Warren, Earl, 24
Warren, Teresa, ix
Wells, David, 104

West Regional Tournament, 74–85
recap, 109–110
television coverage of, 77–78, 80
Williams, Ted, 7, 23, 104
Williamsport, Pennsylvania, xiii, 21, 90
Willis, Wyatt, 94
Winfield, Dave, 7
Withrow, Jim, viii
Woodall, Ian, 92
World Series, Little League. *See* Little
League World Series
Wright, Mickey, 7

X

XX Sports Radio, fundraising by, 86

Y

Yastrzemski, Carl, 22
Yount, Robin, 22

Z

Zizzi, Mike, viii

About the Authors

Mike Ford is coauthor of *Brotherhood of the Pigskin*. He has been involved with youth baseball for over 20 years as a volunteer coach and board member. His résumé includes coaching several championship Little League, Pony, and travel ball teams for his sons Andrew and Daniel. Mike lives with his wife Anne and four children in El Cajon, California.

Wade Lindenberger was born and raised in San Diego, California, where he lives with his wife Kayoko and Pembroke Welsh Corgi Max. An avid Padres fan, he played several years of Little League and high school baseball. Coauthor of *Brotherhood of the Pigskin*, *Blue Bombers* is his first nonfiction book.